JAMESTOWN  EDUCATION

WORLD WORKS™

LEVEL G

LAW ENFORCEMENT

HEALTH

EVERYDAY THINGS

 **Glencoe**

New York, New York   Columbus, Ohio   Chicago, Illinois   Woodland Hills, California

JAMESTOWN EDUCATION

The McGraw·Hill Companies

Send all inquiries to:
Glencoe/McGraw-Hill
8787 Orion Place
Columbus, OH 43240-4027

ISBN: 978-0-07-878020-2
MHID: 0-07-878020-9

Printed in the United States of America.

2 3 4 5 6 7 8 9 10 066 11 10 09 08

Contents

Unit One LAW ENFORCEMENT

Unit Two HEALTH

90

Unit Three EVERYDAY THINGS

To the Student

This book has nine articles that explain how things work or how things are made. In Unit One, you'll read about law enforcement. In Unit Two, you'll learn about health. And in Unit Three, you'll find out more about everyday things.

The articles in this book will make you think. Some of the information in the text may amaze or even shock you. And each article is sure to improve your understanding of how the world works.

As you read this book, you will have the chance to practice six reading skills:

Making Connections   **Finding the Main Idea**
Asking Questions   **Taking Notes**
Visualizing   **Summarizing**

Each lesson in Unit One and Unit Two will focus on one of these reading skills. In Unit Three, each lesson will focus on several of the skills at once.

You will also complete reading comprehension, vocabulary, and writing activities. Many of the activities are similar to the ones on state and national tests. Completing the activities can help you get ready for tests you may have to take later.

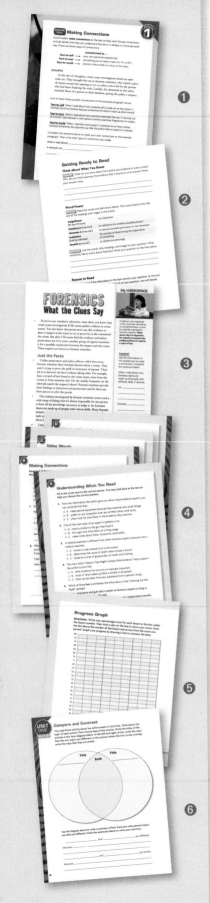

How to Use This Book

About the Book

This book has three units. Each unit has three lessons. Each lesson is built around an article about how something works or how something is made. All the articles have before-reading and after-reading activities.

Working Through Each Lesson

❶ **Reading Skill** Start each lesson by learning a reading skill and getting ready to use it.

❷ **Think About What You Know, Word Power, Reason to Read** Prepare to read the article by completing the activities on this page.

❸ **Article** Read about how something works or how something is made. Enjoy! The activities in the margins will remind you to use the reading skills.

❹ **Activities** Complete activities A, B, C, and D. Then check your work. Your teacher will give you an answer key to do this. Record the number of your correct answers for each activity. At the end of the lesson, add up your total score for activities A, B, and C. Then figure out your percentage score.

❺ **Progress Graph** Record your percentage score on the Progress Graph on page 121.

❻ **Compare and Contrast** Complete the Compare and Contrast activity at the end of each unit. The activity will help you see how the things you read about are alike and different.

Unit 1

Law Enforcement

Forensics

Cybercrime

Police Sketch Artists

FORENSICS
What the Clues Say

Forensic (fə-ren'-sik) scientists examine all kinds of evidence to determine what happened during a crime.

READING SKILL **Making Connections**

Good readers **make connections** to the text as they read. Strong connections include details that help you understand the text in a deeper or more personal way. There are three types of connections.

connects text to . . .

Text-to-self ⟶ your own personal experiences.

Text-to-text ⟶ something you've read or seen on TV or film.

Text-to-world ⟶ events in the world or a story in the news.

EXAMPLE

At the site of a burglary, crime scene investigators found an open soda can. They brought the can to forensic scientists, who wiped a piece of cotton around the opening to try to collect saliva left by the person who had been drinking the soda. Luckily, the chemicals in the saliva matched those of a person in their database, giving the police a suspect.

Look at these three possible connections to the example paragraph above.

Text-to-self When I read about how someone left a soda can at the scene, it reminds me of my brother because sometimes he doesn't clean up after himself.

Text-to-text When I read about how scientists examined the can, it reminds me of a movie I saw because in one scene a scientist examines fingerprints on a glass.

Text-to-world When I read the word *suspect,* it reminds me of news stories because sometimes the reporters say that the police have a suspect in custody.

Complete the sentence below to make your own connection to the example paragraph. Then write what type of connection you made.

When I read about _____

it reminds me _____

_____

because _____

_____

What type of connection did you make? _____

Getting Ready to Read

Think About What You Know

CONNECT What do you know about how police use evidence to solve crimes? Who do you think examines the evidence that is found at crime scenes? Write your answers here.

_____

_____

_____

Word Power

PREVIEW Read the words and definitions below. Then look ahead at the title and at the headings and images in the article.

insignificant (in′-sig-ni′-fi-kənt)	not important
minimize (mi′-nə-mīz′)	to reduce to the smallest possible amount
eliminate (i-li′-mə-nāt′)	to remove something because it's not necessary
evaluation (i-val′-yə-wā′-shən)	the process of determining the importance of something
benefit (be′-nə-fit′)	to receive an advantage

QUESTION Use the words, title, headings, and images to ask a question. What would you like to know about forensics? Write your question on the lines below.

_____

_____

_____

Reason to Read

Read to find out if the information in the text answers your question. At the end of the article, you will be asked to look back at your question. You will decide whether or not your question is answered in the text.

FORENSICS
What the Clues Say

1   If you've ever watched a television crime show, you know that crime scene investigation (CSI) teams gather evidence at crime scenes. You also know that prosecutors use this evidence to place a suspect at the scene to try to prove he or she committed the crime. But after CSI teams find the evidence and before prosecutors use it in court, another group of experts examines it for a possible connection between the suspect and the crime. These experts are known as forensic scientists.

Just the Facts

2   Unlike prosecutors and police officers called detectives, forensic scientists don't develop theories about a crime. They aren't trying to *prove* the guilt or innocence of anyone. Their job is to discover the facts without taking sides. For example, does a strand of hair found at the crime scene come from the victim or from someone else? Do the muddy footprints on the sidewalk match the suspect's shoes? Forensic scientists provide their findings to detectives and prosecutors and let them use these pieces to solve the puzzle.

3   The evidence investigated by forensic scientists covers such a wide range of things that it's almost impossible for one person to have all the knowledge necessary to judge it. So forensics teams are made up of people with various skills. Many forensic scientists specialize in, or concentrate on, one type of evidence, such as poisons, bodily fluids, or fingerprints. (To read more about fingerprints, see *World Works, Level C*, Lesson 9.)

4   Large forensics labs employ scientists with backgrounds in areas such as biology, chemistry, and psychology, to name just a few. Let's take a look at some of these scientists' specialties.

Evidence is very important in the courtroom. But before it is presented there, it must be carefully examined by forensic scientists. **Think about why it's important for experts to examine the evidence before it's used in a court of law.**

Connect

Use the information in the shaded text to make a connection. Complete the sentence below.

When I read about how forensics teams are made up of people with different skills, it reminds

me _____

_____

_____

because _____

_____

_____

What type of connection did you make? You can look back at page 3 for help if you need to.

_____

Aces of Traces

5   Trace evidence experts are masters of detail. At crime scenes, CSI teams collect everything they find, even if it appears to be **insignificant.** The small, seemingly unimportant objects collected—dirt on a rug, a blue fiber in a victim's hair, a fingernail clipping—are known as trace evidence. Sometimes these tiny pieces of information become the key to solving a crime.

6   As they examine trace evidence, these experts try to determine if there's anything unique about an object that can be useful to those investigating the crime. They use a variety of tools, including computers, chemicals, and microscopes, to examine evidence. Sometimes the results produce unexpected leads that can help solve a case. For example, it may turn out that the blue fiber matches the fibers of a suspect's shirt.

7   These experts may also examine a suspect's hands or clothing for traces of gunpowder, which would indicate the person has fired a gun recently. However, most examinations involving **firearms** are handled by another type of forensic scientist called a ballistics expert.

Connect

Use the information in the shaded text to make a connection. Complete the sentence below.

When I read about _____

_____

_____

it reminds me _____

_____

_____

because _____

_____

_____

What type of connection did you make?

_____

When CSI teams find an object like this clothing fiber, they might not be able to tell much from it. But when trace evidence experts examine it under a microscope, they can see details that might match details of other things associated with a suspect. **Think about kinds of fibers that might be found at a crime scene and that might prove to be useful as evidence.**

firearms (fīr′-ärmz′) weapons that use gunpowder to shoot out objects

Bullets Tell Tales

8   One of the main tasks of an expert in ballistics—the study of how bullets and weapons move—is to match a bullet to the gun that fired it. Say a bullet is found at a crime scene, and the police have a suspect who owns a gun that they believe was used in the crime. The ballistics expert fires the gun at a firing range (usually shooting into water or thick fabric to **minimize** the damage to the bullet).

9   The expert examines that bullet under a microscope, noting scratches that were made on it by the gun barrel. Then he or she compares these marks to the marks on the bullet from the crime scene. If the marks are the same, the expert tells the police that the suspect's gun was used to fire the bullet found at the scene.

10   Of course, evidence in a murder investigation includes more than just fibers and bullets. The victim's body also often provides important evidence.

Doctor's Role

11   When a **corpse** is found at a scene, police call a medical examiner (ME). This forensics expert is a doctor who analyzes dead bodies. Unlike other forensics experts, an ME sometimes goes to the crime scene. This is because a corpse, if it is not moved from the scene, can provide clues that only a trained doctor can detect.

12   At the scene, the ME does a quick examination of the corpse, looking for obvious signs of violence. Then he or she estimates the time of death by taking the body's temperature, checking for **rigor mortis,** and looking for purple marks that suggest the blood has settled. While it's impossible to figure out the exact time of death, knowing the approximate time of death is important because it might **eliminate** a suspect who was someplace else when the crime occurred.

---

corpse (kôrps) a dead body
rigor mortis (ri′-gər-môr′-təs) the condition in which muscles become stiff and almost unmovable after death

Connect
Use the information in the shaded text to make a connection. Complete the sentence below.

When I read about how there are some things that only a doctor can figure out, it reminds me

_____

_____

_____

because _____

_____

_____

What type of connection did you make?

_____

7

Most of an ME's work is done at a special lab called a morgue. **Think about why there is a separate lab for examining dead bodies.**

Connect

Reread **paragraph 14**. Use the information in the text to make a strong connection.

_____

_____

_____

_____

_____

_____

_____

What type of connection did you make?

_____

13   If the ME suspects that the cause of death was not natural, he or she sends the body to a special lab called a morgue. At the morgue the ME performs an autopsy, which is a detailed inspection of a dead body to determine the cause of death. After collecting trace evidence from the body (including anything found under the fingernails), the ME examines both the outside and inside of the victim's body to look for signs of violence, such as cuts, bruises, or punctures. After the examination, the ME decides whether the death was natural, an accident, or a **homicide,** in which case detectives and prosecutors will then investigate what happened to the victim.

ABCs of DNA

14   One type of evidence that has become increasingly important in recent years is DNA, the chemicals in a person's body that determine its traits and how it works. Because DNA is found in almost all of a person's cells, it can be taken from any substance from a person's body—a strand of hair, a fingernail clipping, and even saliva. While most of what makes up DNA is similar in all people, forensic scientists are interested in the small part of the chemical that varies between people.

15   As experts focus on the part of DNA that varies, they decide whether or not DNA found at a crime scene matches a suspect's DNA. If they find similarities and call it a match, it does not necessarily mean the two DNA samples are from the same person. But the chance of one person's DNA matching another person's is one in hundreds of millions—or even billions. This gives DNA evidence great weight in the courtroom.

homicide (hä′-mə-sīd′) the crime of one person killing another

Objects That Might Contain DNA Evidence		
Evidence	Location of DNA on Evidence	Where DNA Came From
hat	inside the object	sweat, hair, dandruff
eyeglasses	nosepiece or earpieces, lenses	sweat, skin
stamp or envelope	area on back that was licked	saliva
can	sides, opening	saliva, sweat
blanket	surface	sweat, hair, saliva

Source: National Institute of Justice, © 1999

The chart above shows a few common objects that might contain DNA. **Think about other common objects that might contain DNA and what the source of the DNA might be.**

Nothing but the Truth

16   Forensic scientists themselves are often called to testify in court. They're known as expert witnesses because their testimony is based on their scientific **evaluation**—not their opinion—of the evidence. To be an effective witness, a forensic scientist must be able to explain complex scientific tests in terms that nonscientific people on the jury can understand.

17   And prosecutors aren't the only ones who make use of forensics results. Sometimes the **defense** can **benefit** from the findings of forensics experts as well. Because forensics experts focus solely on the facts, they're as helpful in proving innocence as they are in proving guilt. This means forensic scientists are important not just to police and prosecutors but to justice overall.

defense (di-fens') in a court case, the person or persons accused of a crime and the lawyers who try to prove that the person or persons are not guilty

Self-Check
Look back at the question you wrote on page 4.
- Does the information in the text answer your question? If it does, what is the answer? If it does not, where could you look to find more information?
Write your answers on a separate sheet of paper.

Understanding What You Read

Fill in the circle next to the correct answer. You may look back at the text to help you choose the correct answers.

1. From the information the author gave you about trace evidence experts, you can conclude that they
   - ○ A. need special equipment because they examine very small things.
   - ○ B. prefer to use computers over any of their other work tools.
   - ○ C. often look for blue fibers in the evidence they examine.

2. One of the main tasks of an expert in ballistics is to
   - ○ A. match a bullet to the gun that fired it.
   - ○ B. fire a gun into thick fabric at a firing range.
   - ○ C. make notes about fibers, footprints, and bullets.

3. A medical examiner is different from other forensics experts because only a medical examiner
   - ○ A. works in a lab instead of at crime scenes.
   - ○ B. determines the cause of death when a body is found.
   - ○ C. looks for traces of gunpowder on hands and clothing.

4. The chart titled "Objects That Might Contain DNA Evidence" helps support the author's point that
   - ○ A. DNA evidence has become increasingly important.
   - ○ B. most of what makes up DNA is similar in all people.
   - ○ C. DNA can be taken from any substance from a person's body.

5. Which of these **best** summarizes the information in the "Nothing but the Truth" section?
   - ○ A. Innocence and guilt don't matter to forensics experts as long as justice is served in the end.
   - ○ B. Forensics experts need to explain some very complicated scientific ideas in language that everyone can understand.
   - ○ C. Both prosecutors and defense lawyers can use forensics experts as witnesses in court to testify about their findings.

Score 4 points for each correct answer.

_____/20 **Total Score: Activity A**

Making Connections

Paragraph 16 from the article is shown below. Read the paragraph. Then use the paragraph to complete the activities.

> Forensic scientists themselves are often called to testify in court. They're known as expert witnesses because their testimony is based on their scientific evaluation—not their opinion—of the evidence. To be an effective witness, a forensic scientist must be able to explain complex scientific tests in terms that nonscientific people on the jury can understand.

1. Complete the sentence to make a connection to the paragraph above.

When I read about _____

_____

it reminds me _____

_____

because _____

_____

2. What type of connection did you make to the paragraph above? How do you know? Write your answers below. You can look back at page 3 for help if you need to.

Type of Connection _____

How I Know _____

_____

_____

Score 5 points each for numbers 1 and 2.

_____ /10 **Total Score: Activity B**

Using Words

The words and phrases in the list below relate to the words in the box. Some words or phrases in the list are synonyms. They have the same meaning. Some words or phrases are antonyms. They have the opposite meaning. Write the related word from the box on each line. Use each word from the box **twice.**

insignificant	minimize	eliminate
evaluation	benefit	

Synonyms

1. judgment of value _____

2. decrease _____

3. minor _____

4. rule out _____

5. profit _____

6. study of worth _____

Antonyms

7. include _____

8. be hindered _____

9. boost _____

10. vital _____

Score 2 points for each correct answer.

_____ /20   **Total Score: Activity C**

Writing About It

Write a Postcard Suppose your class went on a field trip to a lab where forensic scientists work. Write a postcard to a friend. Tell your friend what you learned about forensics. Finish the sentences below to write your postcard. Be sure your writing matches the information in the text. Use the checklist on page 119 to check your work.

Dear _____

    Today our class visited forensic scientists. Forensic

scientists are _____

We met some trace evidence experts who were using

microscopes to _____

Then we met a medical examiner. Her job is _____

_____

All the forensics experts we met stressed that their job

is not to form opinions but to _____

_____

    Sincerely,

_____

123 Evidence Lane
Anytown, State 54321

Lesson 1 Add your scores from activities A, B, and C to get your total score.

_____ **A** Understanding What You Read
_____ **B** Making Connections
_____ **C** Using Words
_____ **Total Score**

Multiply your **Total Score x 2** _____
This is your percentage score.
Record your percentage score on the graph on page 121.

CYBERCRIME
CRIMINALS ON THE INTERNET

Many criminals use the Internet
to commit illegal acts.

READING SKILL | Asking Questions

Good readers check their thoughts as they read by asking themselves questions. **Asking questions** can help you find out what you do and do not understand. If you aren't able to answer a question you've asked yourself, you can use fix-up strategies to help you. Below is a list of possible fix-up strategies. Try using them, and choose the ones that work best for you.

EXAMPLE

In 2007 a student in Pennsylvania was arrested for changing information in school files. The student used his computer to gain access to school records. He changed the grades of five of his friends. The student could be sentenced to up to five years' probation for this crime.

Look at the self-check questions and fix-up strategies shown below.

Self-Check Questions

- How would I explain the meaning of what I just read?
- How can I restate what the author is saying so that it makes sense to me?
- How would I explain the most important ideas in the text?
- How would I summarize the information I just read?

Fix-Up Strategies

- **Reread** part of the text.
- **Make a connection** to the information in the text.
- **Find the meaning** of words you don't understand.
- **Take notes.**

- **Visualize** the information in the text.
- **Draw** a web, chart, or picture of the ideas in the text.
- **Ask** your teacher or another student for help.

Write a self-check question to check your understanding of the example paragraph. Then answer your question. If you have trouble, use one or more of the fix-up strategies to help you.

Self-Check Question _____

Answer _____

Fix-Up Strategies _____

Getting Ready to Read

Think About What You Know

CONNECT Think about all the different ways to use the Internet. What do you know about how criminals use the Internet to commit crimes? Write your answer here.

_____

_____

_____

Word Power

PREVIEW Read the words and definitions below. Then look ahead at the title and at the headings and images in the article.

widespread (wīd′-spred′)	happening in many places and among many people
proficiency (prə-fi′-shən-sē)	the ability to do something well
update (əp′-dāt′)	to make sure the information for something is current and accurate
highlight (hī′-līt′)	to direct special attention to something
deleted (di-lēt′-əd)	erased

PREDICT Use the words, title, headings, and images to make a prediction. What do you think the author will say about cybercrime?

I predict the author will _____

_____

because _____

_____

Reason to Read

Read to find out if the prediction you wrote above matches the information in the text. At the end of the article, you will be asked about your prediction. You will need to explain how your prediction is the same as the text or different from it.

CYBERCRIME
CRIMINALS ON THE INTERNET

1   In 2006 a businesswoman in Kentucky received an e-mail from the bank her company used. The e-mail stated that the bank needed information from the company. She promptly replied, sending the information. Unfortunately, the e-mail was sent by thieves, not the bank. The thieves used an e-mail scheme to trick the businesswoman, and then they stole more than $163,000 from her company's bank accounts. The businesswoman and her company were victims of a form of crime called cybercrime, in which criminals use computers and the Internet to commit illegal acts.

Computer Crimes

2   Whether they're snatching purses or going through people's garbage to steal credit card numbers, criminals are always looking for easier ways to access other people's money. In recent years, the **widespread** use of personal computers has given thieves a whole new method of getting money.

3   Some cybercriminals use the computer to commit only traditional crimes. Fraud, or tricks a thief plays in order to get someone's money, is one example. Before computers, fraud might have involved someone going door-to-door selling land that didn't really exist. Now, by using a computer, that same criminal can make the sales pitch by sending one e-mail to thousands of people at once instead of speaking to them one by one.

4   The Internet also allows criminals to be invisible when they commit fraud. Criminals can use stolen credit card numbers right from their keyboards instead of going to an actual store. Internet stores can't check to see if a user's signature matches the signature on the back of the card, and they can't check photo identification. Because they're not buying things in person, cybercriminals are well hidden.

Ask Questions

Ask yourself, "How would I explain the most important ideas in **paragraph 4**?"

How would using the fix-up strategy of drawing a main idea web help you answer the question?

_____

_____

_____

_____

How would using the fix-up strategy of making a connection help you answer the question?

_____

_____

_____

_____

Ask Questions

Ask yourself a self-check question about **paragraph 6.** Look back at the questions listed on page 15 if you need to. Write your question below.

_____

_____

_____

What fix-up strategies could you use to answer your question? Write your answer and your fix-up strategies below.

Answer_____

_____

_____

_____

Fix-Up Strategies _____

_____

_____

_____

Secure

Companies use symbols such as a lock to let you know it's safe to enter personal information. **Think about what kinds of Web sites offer this protection.**

5   Stealing credit card numbers is just one example of identity theft, an old crime that takes a new approach in the age of the Internet.

When Someone Else Is You

6   When criminals commit identity theft, they get hold of personal information such as a credit card number or a bank password and use it to commit fraud. Criminals especially like stealing a person's social security number (SSN), the number that government agencies and banks use to identify that person. If criminals get your SSN, they've gotten your most important financial password. With just your credit card number or bank account information, criminals can buy things and leave you with the bill or transfer money from your accounts. The damage they can do with your SSN, though, is much greater— they can run up massive amounts of **debt** in your name by purchasing cars and even homes.

7   Tons of banking and shopping is done **online,** and more and more people are sending personal information over the Internet. That's fine as long as the information goes only to the Web site of the appropriate company or store. But what if thieves with computer **proficiency** gain access to private information on that Web site? There's no need for them to steal credit card numbers from the trash when they can steal them online. They can do this by hacking, which is the act of breaking into a computer. If they hack into an online store's computers, they can access the information you're sending.

8   Most Web sites that take personal information provide protection through encryption. The encryption process converts your typed information into a secret code. This makes your personal information secure. At an encrypted site, your information can only be viewed by those who have the code.

---

debt (det) an amount that is owed
online (ôn'-līn') connected to a computer system such as the Internet

Go Phish

9   Another method cybercriminals use to get information and money is a process called phishing. Phishing involves sending e-mails or setting up Web sites to try to trick people into giving out personal information.

10   The story of the Kentucky businesswoman is an example of phishing. A professional-looking e-mail requests that you **update** your personal information at a bank's Web site; the e-mail will even contain a **link** for you to click. The site the link takes you to looks like the bank's site, but it's really a fake one set up by the criminals. You probably won't notice anything unusual, so you think it's safe to type in your personal information. Then the criminals have your information to use however they want.

Ask Questions

Ask yourself a self-check question about **paragraph 10**. Write your question below.

_____

_____

_____

What fix-up strategies could you use to answer your question? Write your answer and your fix-up strategies below.

Answer _____

_____

_____

_____

Fix-Up Strategies _____

_____

_____

_____

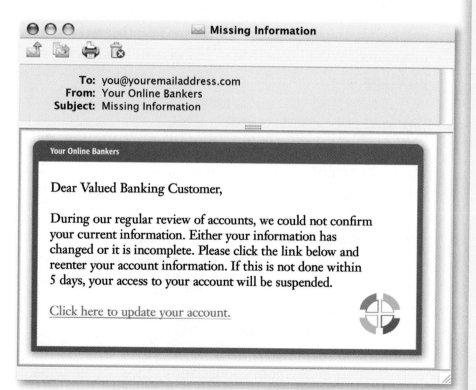

The illustration above shows what a phishing e-mail might look like. **Think about why people can be easily tricked by phishing e-mails.**

link (lingk) text or an image in an e-mail or on a Web site that connects to another Web site or page when clicked

Not Just the Money

11   Not all cybercrime is just a **hi-tech** way to steal money. Sometimes cybercriminals use the Internet and computers for other illegal—and sometimes very dangerous—activities.

12   Developing and spreading computer viruses is a common cybercriminal activity. These viruses can, among other things, slow down a computer's performance and erase its data. Because they're able to make copies of themselves, viruses often spread quickly between computers, destroying important information and costing companies millions of dollars.

13   Hacking can be destructive too. Hackers might break into an electric company's computers to cause blackouts. Or they might break into government computers to steal secret information. Sometimes hackers even endanger human lives. In 2004, for example, hackers in Romania gained access to computers controlling the life-support system for scientists working in Antarctica. While no lives were lost, this incident does **highlight** how serious the consequences of cybercrime can be.

Connect

Reread **paragraph 12.** Use the information in the text to make a connection. Complete the sentence below.

When I read about _____

_____

_____

it reminds me _____

_____

_____

because _____

_____

_____

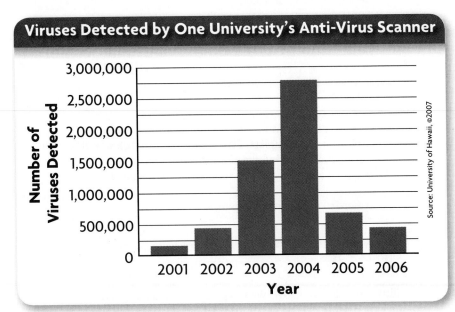

Viruses Detected by One University's Anti-Virus Scanner

Number of Viruses Detected vs. Year

Source: University of Hawaii, ©2007

Most computers and networks use anti-virus software for protection against infection. **Think about why it's important to update this software regularly.**

hi-tech (hī-tek′) referring to advanced computers or technology

Ways to Fight Cybercrime

14   Because so many people all over the world now have computers with access to the Internet, it is difficult for law enforcement to combat cybercrime. Hackers in one country can break into computers in other countries, and it's hard for police to crack down on criminals hidden across the world. But even though criminals keep finding new ways to use the Internet, law enforcement does have some effective methods it can use to fight back.

15   One of the most useful methods is the ability to locate the specific computer used in a crime. Every computer has its own electronic "footprint," which is a number assigned to it when it connects to the Internet. Every e-mail that is sent contains this footprint. Police can follow this number straight to the guilty computer. The police then take the computer and examine it to see what files have been **deleted,** what e-mails have been sent or received, and so on.

16   You too can help fight cybercrime by protecting yourself when you're online:

- Never send personal information to Web sites that are not encrypted.
- Never open an e-mail unless you know who sent it.
- Never download a file unless you trust the source.

17   Following these guidelines may not keep you completely safe, but it will help ensure that you're not making it easier for cybercriminals to commit their crimes.

Once they seize a computer that was used to commit a crime, the police can get lots of information from it. **Think about what information a computer might have that would be useful to police.**

Self-Check
Look back at the prediction you wrote on page 16.
- Does your prediction match the information in the text? Why or why not?
Write your answers on a separate sheet of paper.

Understanding What You Read

Fill in the circle next to the correct answer. You may look back at the text to help you choose the correct answers.

1. At an encrypted site, your information can only be viewed by
- ○ A. cybercriminals.
- ○ B. those who have the code.
- ○ C. law enforcement officers.

2. What is one effect of cybercriminals' sending of phishing e-mails?
- ○ A. A person's computer starts to work very slowly.
- ○ B. Hackers can access secret government information.
- ○ C. Police can follow the "footprint" in the e-mails to the computer that sent them.

3. Under which heading from the article would you **most likely** find information about identity theft?
- ○ A. When Someone Else Is You
- ○ B. Not Just the Money
- ○ C. Go Phish

4. The bar graph titled "Viruses Detected by One University's Anti-Virus Scanner" helps support the author's point that computer viruses
- ○ A. are a popular tool among cybercriminals.
- ○ B. spread easily from computer to computer.
- ○ C. can destroy important information on a computer.

5. From the information the author gave you about cybercrime, you can conclude that
- ○ A. in the future, cybercrime will no longer exist.
- ○ B. cybercriminals are rarely punished for their crimes.
- ○ C. police will continue to find new ways to fight cybercrime.

Score 4 points for each correct answer.

_____ /20   **Total Score: Activity A**

Asking Questions

Paragraph 15 from the article is shown below. Read the paragraph. Then use the paragraph to complete the activities.

One of the most useful methods is the ability to locate the specific computer used in a crime. Every computer has its own electronic "footprint," which is a number assigned to it when it connects to the Internet. Every e-mail that is sent contains this footprint. Police can follow this number straight to the guilty computer. The police then take the computer and examine it to see what files have been deleted, what e-mails have been sent or received, and so on.

1. Fill in the circle next to the **best** self-check question to ask after reading the paragraph.
   - ○ A. How do I find out what an electronic footprint looks like?
   - ○ B. How can I learn more about how police recover files that have been deleted?
   - ○ C. How would I explain the meaning of what I just read about police locating computers used in crimes?

2. Write another question to check your understanding of the paragraph. Then write the answer to your question and the fix-up strategies you used.

   Self-Check Question _____

   _____

   Answer _____

   _____

   Fix-Up Strategies _____

   _____

Score 5 points each for numbers 1 and 2.

_____ /10 **Total Score: Activity B**

Using Words

Follow the instructions below. Write your answers on the lines.

1. List **three** things that could cause **widespread** damage.

   _____

   _____

   _____

2. List **two** things that people are usually able to do if they have **proficiency** in music.

   _____

   _____

3. List **two** reasons why a school might want to **update** their student files.

   _____

   _____

4. List **two** ways a teacher might **highlight** information for students.

   _____

   _____

5. List **two** reasons why someone's e-mail address might be **deleted** from a person's address book.

   _____

   _____

Score 4 points for each correct answer.

_____ /20   **Total Score: Activity C**

Writing About It

Write a Speech Suppose someone asks you to give a speech about cybercrime. Write a speech that tells people how to avoid becoming victims of cybercrime. Finish the sentences below to write your speech. Be sure your writing matches the information in the text. Use the checklist on page 119 to check your work.

I'm here today to warn you about the dangers of cybercrime. Cybercrime is

_____

_____

The Internet makes it easier for criminals to steal because _____

_____

You must make sure thieves do not have access to your personal information,

such as your social security number, because _____

_____

One way criminals get people's personal information and money is by phishing,

which is _____

_____

You can help protect yourself online by _____

_____

_____

_____

Lesson 2 Add your scores from activities A, B, and C to get your total score.
_____ **A** Understanding What You Read
_____ **B** Asking Questions
_____ **C** Using Words
_____ **Total Score**

Multiply your **Total Score x 2** _____
This is your percentage score.
Record your percentage score on the graph on page 121.

POLICE SKETCH
ARTISTS
The Art of Fighting Crime

CITY POLICE

Sketch artists use their creativity to help police solve crimes.

 **Visualizing**

Good readers use their imagination and all of their senses as they read. They use details from the text and what they already know to **visualize** what they are reading. Authors may include details about color, shape, size, and movement to describe how things look. They may also include details about how things smell, feel, sound, and taste. Visualizing can help you understand the text. It can also help you remember more of what you read.

EXAMPLE

When an artist sketches a person's face, the artist usually does not use an ordinary pencil. Artists carefully select their pencils according to what kinds of lines they want to draw. A pencil with a softer core is good for making broad, or wide, strokes, such as the shadow a person's nose casts on his or her face. A pencil with a harder core is good for making fine, or thin, lines, such as wrinkles or eyelashes.

From the information in the example paragraph above, what do you think it looks, feels, and sounds like to be an artist making a pencil sketch? The details *broad, or wide, strokes* and *fine, or thin, lines* can help you visualize this. What would the different kinds of lines look like? How would it feel to make these lines on paper? What would the pencils sound like as they're moved across the paper?

Draw a picture of what you are visualizing in the box below. Include as many details as possible in your drawing.

Getting Ready to Read

Think About What You Know

CONNECT Think about how hard it can be to draw a person's face so that it looks just like him or her. How does an artist use one person's description to make a drawing of another person? What kinds of details do you think help the artist make the drawing? Write your answers here.

_____

_____

_____

Word Power

PREVIEW Read the words and definitions below. Then look ahead at the title and at the headings and images in the article.

feedback (fēd'-bak')	comments made in response to something that's been done
omitted (ō-mit'-əd)	left something out, either on purpose or by accident
incorporated (in-kôr'-pə-rāt'-əd)	joined with something else to form a new whole
receding (ri-sēd'-ing)	moving back from an original location
invaluable (in-val'-yə-bəl)	having great value or use

QUESTION Use the words, title, headings, and images to ask a question. What would you like to know about police sketch artists? Write your question on the lines below.

_____

_____

_____

Reason to Read

Read to find out if the information in the text answers your question. At the end of the article, you will be asked to look back at your question. You will decide whether or not your question is answered in the text.

POLICE SKETCH ARTISTS
The Art of Fighting Crime

1   Close your eyes. Try to accurately describe the face of your best friend. Think about the shape of your friend's eyes and forehead, or about the size of his or her nose. Can you do it? What if you had to describe the face of a stranger who just passed you on the street?

2   Police sketch artists count on people being able to describe other people. Listening to random details provided by witnesses to crimes and putting them together to make an accurate sketch is all part of a day's work.

Art and Science

3   The main task of police sketch artists is to produce a detailed image of an unknown person. They might use pencil and paper or a computer to produce an image, or they might use clay to make a **three-dimensional** model of a person's face. In fact, because police sketch artists sometimes use tools other than just pencil and paper, it's more accurate to call them forensic artists.

4   The forensic artist's goal is to create something that will help police do their work. These are some of the most common tasks of a forensic artist:

- Sketching a suspect in a crime
- Creating a model to help identify a skeleton
- Updating an image of a person who has been missing for years

5   But whatever the task, forensic artists bring a variety of skills to their work.

---

three-dimensional (thrē′-də-mench′-nəl) having length, depth, and height

This sketch of the terrorist known as the Unabomber was shown across the country during the search for the suspect. **Think about why police would want to show the image of a suspect all over the country.**

Visualize

Reread the shaded text. Use the details in the text to imagine the face of your best friend.

Draw what you are visualizing in the box below.

6   Obviously, forensic artists need artistic abilities—after all, an image will help only if it's done well. Some of their duties also require a background in scientific areas such as **anatomy.** And they must be good interviewers. This is particularly important in one of the most common duties of a forensic artist: suspect identification.

Witness's Words

7   Suppose someone broke into a store. The only clue the police have is a woman who saw the burglar pass her on the street. The forensic artist needs to produce a sketch of the suspect based on the witness's description.

8   The forensic artist begins by asking general questions such as *How much light was in the street?* This allows the witness to relax and to describe the event in his or her own words. It also helps the witness trust his or her own memory. The forensic artist then moves on to questions about the suspect's appearance, usually starting with head size and eventually asking about age, **complexion,** hairstyle, eye color, tattoos, and so on. By encouraging the witness to focus on smaller details one at a time, the witness feels less pressure and can focus better. For example, asking the witness to focus on the suspect's eyebrows encourages the witness to think about whether they were bushy, normal, or plucked. Often the artist shows the witness photographs of general facial features to help the witness focus.

Pencil, Plastic, and Programs

9   As the witness describes each feature, the artist draws. The witness is asked for **feedback** and can suggest changes as the drawing and interviewing process goes along. For example, the witness might say that the eyes drawn by the artist are too close together, or he or she might realize that a detail such as a scar was **omitted.**

anatomy (ə-na′-tə-mē) the study of body structure
complexion (kəm-plek′-shən) the color or appearance of the skin, usually of the face

Visualize

Reread the shaded text. Write **two** details from the text that help you visualize the author's description of how eyebrows might look.

1. _____

2. _____

What would you have to already know to be able to use these details to visualize?

_____

_____

_____

_____

30

10   Sometimes the artist puts aside pencil and paper and uses clear plastic sheets placed on top of each other. These sheets are called foils, and each one shows a facial feature such as a nose or cheekbones. The artist flips through the nose foils until the witness says, "Yes, that looks right." Then the artist flips through the foils for the other features, placing sheets with features confirmed by the witness on top of one another, until there is a whole picture of the suspect's face. Sometimes the artist uses computer programs that do something very similar.

11   After the witness says there is a strong resemblance between the image and the suspect, the image is displayed in public places and on news networks. The hope is that by making the image public, someone will recognize the person and contact the police with information.

Bone to Flesh

12   When a skeleton is discovered, police try to figure out the dead person's identity by matching the skeleton's teeth to dental records or by checking for **DNA** matches. Police sometimes ask a forensic artist to make a reconstruction, or model, of the person's face.

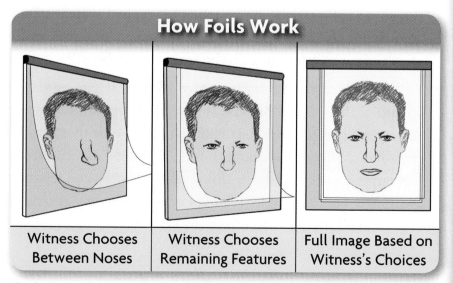

How Foils Work

| Witness Chooses Between Noses | Witness Chooses Remaining Features | Full Image Based on Witness's Choices |

Think about why focusing on each feature results in a more accurate picture.

DNA (dē′-en′-ā′) chemicals found in cells, such as in skin or hair cells, that can be used to identify the person the cells came from

Connect

Reread **paragraph 11.** Use the information in the text to make a connection. Complete the sentence below.

When I read about how the image is displayed in public places, it reminds me

_____

_____

_____

because _____

_____

_____

By using a variety of scientific research, the artist decides how much clay to use based on the victim's age, gender, and race. **Think about how a younger person's flesh might appear different from an older person's.**

Connect

Reread the shaded text. Use the information in the text to make a connection. Complete the sentence below.

When I read about _____

_____

_____

_____

it reminds me _____

_____

_____

_____

because _____

_____

_____

_____

13   The reconstruction is a two-phase operation that combines scientific examination with art. By examining the bones, medical scientists can usually provide information about the person's age, race, and gender. For example, the size of some bones tends to differ between men and women, and the condition of an elderly person's bones is different from that of a young adult's bones. The forensic artist combines this information with information from a special scientific chart that shows muscle and skin differences by age, race, and gender.

14   Next the artist uses all this information and modeling clay to build a three-dimensional face, placing the clay directly onto the skull. The artist even puts artificial eyes into the sculpture. The finished sculpture is photographed, and the photos are compared to pictures of people listed as missing to see if any of them match.

Then and Now

15   What happens if police are looking for a person who's been missing for many years? A person's appearance changes over time, so old photographs aren't always accurate. Luckily, forensic artists' understanding of science and art helps them create an age-progression sketch. This type of sketch is used mostly for children who have been missing a long time or for **fugitives** who have been on the run for years.

16   Often the artist has nothing to work with but an outdated photo of the subject. Because the artist understands how aging changes a person's face, he or she can guess how that person's face has changed. For example, for a missing child, the artist accounts for the fact that a child's face broadens and lengthens with age. Photos of older relatives of the child may also be studied and **incorporated** into the sketch.

fugitives (fū′-jə-tivs) people who are illegally avoiding police capture

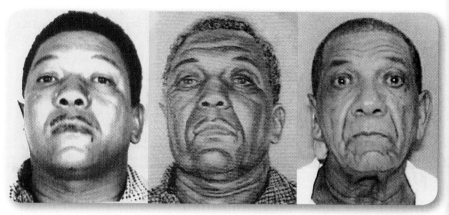

A fugitive's appearance might change a lot over the years, so sketch artists update the image (as in the middle picture above) to help the police. **Think about ways a fugitive might try to change his or her appearance.**

17   For missing adults or fugitives, the artist considers signs of aging such as thinning lips and a **receding** hairline. The artist also considers the subject's habits. For example, the face of someone who smokes will age more quickly than a nonsmoker's face.

18   Meanwhile, fugitives might try to change their appearance by growing a beard, gaining weight, or dyeing their hair. To cover all the possibilities, a forensic artist will produce multiple images of the fugitive.

19   As you can see, it's no small task to create something complete with very little information—and to put a face to the unknown. If it's true that a picture is worth a thousand words, then forensic artists are truly **invaluable** members of law enforcement teams.

Did You Know?

When they do reconstructions from skeletons, artists often factor in objects found with the skeleton.

- Glasses may be added to the model.
- A long belt may indicate the person was heavyset.
- Pieces of hair suggest what kind of wig to use on the model.

My WORKSPACE

Visualize

Reread **paragraph 18.** Write **two** details from the text that help you visualize ways fugitives might change their looks.

1. _____

   _____

2. _____

   _____

Use the details in the text and what you already know to visualize a fugitive before and after his or her appearance changes. Draw what you are visualizing below.

Self-Check

Look back at the question you wrote on page 28.

- Does the information in the text answer your question? If it does, what is the answer? If it does not, where could you look to find more information?

Write your answers on a separate sheet of paper.

Understanding What You Read

Fill in the circle next to the correct answer. You may look back at the text to help you choose the correct answers.

1. The main task of police sketch artists is to produce
   - ○ A. a detailed image of an unknown person.
   - ○ B. a chart showing age, race, and gender.
   - ○ C. trust between police and witnesses.

2. Which step has to happen **before** the artist makes a sketch of a suspect in a crime?
   - ○ A. The police arrest the suspect.
   - ○ B. The witness describes the suspect.
   - ○ C. The suspect's family provides photos of relatives.

3. The diagram titled "How Foils Work" helps support the author's point that
   - ○ A. each plastic sheet shows one feature.
   - ○ B. artists also use computer programs.
   - ○ C. police sketches help solve crimes.

4. What problem does an age-progression sketch help solve?
   - ○ A. Witnesses often have trouble trusting their own memory.
   - ○ B. Sometimes people find skeletons without any identification.
   - ○ C. People who have been missing for years probably look different from their old pictures.

5. The information in the "Did You Know?" box on page 33 gives you
   - ○ A. new information about making sketches.
   - ○ B. the most important ideas from the article.
   - ○ C. details about one of forensic artists' tasks.

Score 4 points for each correct answer.

_____/20   **Total Score: Activity A**

Visualizing

Paragraph 11 from the article is shown below. Read the paragraph. Then use the paragraph to complete the activities.

> After the witness says there is a strong resemblance between the image and the suspect, the image is displayed in public places and on news networks. The hope is that by making the image public, someone will recognize the person and contact the police with information.

1. Which details from the paragraph help you visualize how forensic artists' sketches are used? How does what you already know from using your senses help you visualize this? Write your answers below.

Detail _____

Detail _____

Detail _____

What I Know _____

_____

2. Use the details from the above paragraph, what you already know, and your imagination to create a picture in your mind. Draw what you are visualizing in the box below. Make sure your drawing matches the details in the text.

Score 5 points each for numbers 1 and 2.

_____ /10   **Total Score: Activity B**

Using Words

Complete each sentence with a word from the box. Write the missing word on the line.

> **feedback**   **omitted**   **incorporated**
> **receding**   **invaluable**

1. Knowing how to swim is one of many _____ skills a person must have to be a lifeguard.

2. When my friend was telling me about the movie she just saw, she

   _____ the surprise scary ending.

3. After the flood, the _____ water left some fields very muddy.

4. My teacher gave me some helpful _____ on the draft of my paper.

5. The builder _____ all of our ideas into a complete design for the new house.

Choose one word from the box. Write a new sentence using the word. Be sure to put at least one detail in your sentence. The detail should show that you understand what the word means. Use the sentences above as examples.

6. _____

   _____

Score 4 points for each correct answer in numbers 1–5.
(Do not score number 6.)
_____ /20   **Total Score: Activity C**

Writing About It

Write a Journal Entry Suppose your class took a field trip to see a police sketch artist in action. Write a journal entry about your field trip. Finish the sentences below to write your journal entry. Include details about what you saw, heard, and felt. Be sure your writing matches the information in the text. Use the checklist on page 119 to check your work.

Today my class visited forensic artists at the local police station. We learned

that the work of a police sketch artist is important because _____

_____

_____

One of the sketch artists was interviewing a witness to _____

_____

As the artist asked questions, she _____

_____

We also saw another artist take a skull and _____

_____

Seeing the different things the artists were doing made

us realize _____

_____

_____

Lesson 3 Add your scores from activities A, B, and C to get your total score.

_____ **A** Understanding What You Read
_____ **B** Visualizing
_____ **C** Using Words
_____ **Total Score**

Multiply your **Total Score x 2** _____
This is your percentage score.
Record your percentage score on the graph on page 121.

Compare and Contrast

You read three articles about law enforcement in Unit One. Think about the topic of each article. Then choose **two** of the articles. Write the titles of the articles in the Venn diagram below. In the left and right circles, write the ways that the two topics are different. In the section where the two circles overlap, write the ways that they are similar.

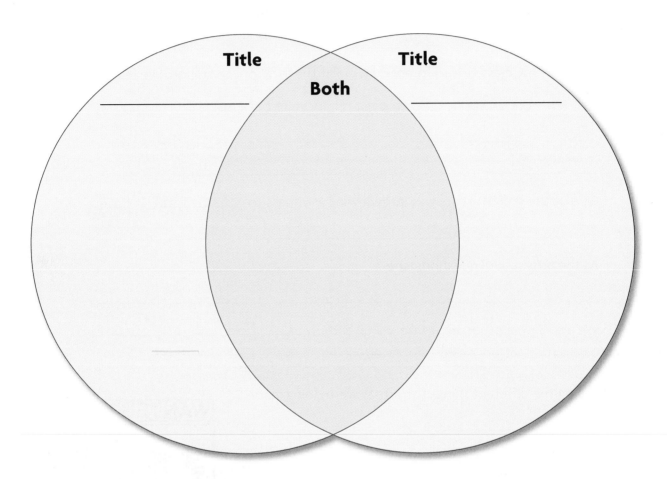

Title _____

Both

Title _____

Use the diagram above to write a summary of how these law enforcement topics are alike and different. Finish the sentences below to write your summary.

_____ and _____ are different

because _____

_____

_____ and _____ are similar

because _____

_____

Unit 2

Health

Infectious Diseases

Aspirin

Anthrax

ASPIRIN
The Wonder Drug

Aspirin was one of the first pain
medicines. But today people use
it for more than just pain relief.

Finding the Main Idea and Details

The most important idea in a text is the **main idea.** The main idea is always a general idea. The supporting **details** are more specific. They give detailed information about the main idea. Good readers know how to infer, or determine, the main idea from the text even when there isn't a topic sentence. To infer the main idea of a paragraph, study the details in the paragraph to figure out what they have in common. You can use this information and your own knowledge to determine the main idea.

An inferred main idea can be close to the text (made up of words already in the text) or far from the text (made up of mostly new words that form a bigger idea).

EXAMPLE

Have you ever had a headache? Headaches are more common in adults, but many kids get headaches too. Researchers have found that headaches in young people are sometimes related to stressful school experiences. Taking a long exam, working on a difficult assignment, or having a conflict with a classmate all might trigger a headache.

Here are some of the important details from the example paragraph:

Kids get headaches too.

Headaches in young people are sometimes related to stressful school experiences.

A long exam, a difficult assignment, or a conflict with a classmate all might trigger a headache.

What do these details have in common? They all focus on headaches and why young people might get them. Use this information to infer the main idea of the paragraph. Write the main idea below.

_____

_____

Is the main idea you wrote close to the text or far from the text? Why?

_____

_____

Getting Ready to Read

Think About What You Know

CONNECT Think about the last time a part of your body was in pain. How did it affect you? Did you do anything to try to relieve the pain? If so, what did you do? Write your answers here.

_____

_____

_____

Word Power

PREVIEW Read the words and definitions below. Then look ahead at the title and at the headings and images in the article.

extracted (ik-strakt′-əd)	carefully removed using a machine or a chemical process
ingested (in-jest′-əd)	taken into the body by eating or drinking
debilitating (di-bi′-lə-tāt′-ing)	causing illness or the loss of strength
chronic (krä′-nik)	lasting for a long time or happening frequently
correlation (kôr′-ə-lā′-shən)	a connection between ideas or events that suggests one might be the cause of the other

PREDICT Use the words, title, headings, and images to make a prediction. What do you think the author will say about aspirin?

I predict the author will _____

_____

because _____

_____

Reason to Read

Read to find out if the prediction you wrote above matches the information in the text. At the end of the article, you will be asked about your prediction. You will need to explain how your prediction is the same as the text or different from it.

ASPIRIN
The Wonder Drug

1   If you have ever had a mild but painful injury, such as a strained muscle, your doctor may have recommended an **over-the-counter** pain reliever. Today there are many different pain-relief medications available at the drugstore. Most of them have one thing in common: they are the descendants of aspirin.

2   Millions of adults use aspirin as a remedy for headaches, backaches, swelling, and a variety of other pains. Let's see how this tiny pill provides such great relief.

Pain Relief from a Plant

3   More than 2,000 years ago, doctors knew that a bitter powder **extracted** from the bark of the willow tree could ease a person's pain when **ingested.** Centuries later, scientists began to isolate the specific pain-relieving substance in willow bark. Unfortunately, this substance caused negative **side effects** for the people who took it: it upset the stomach and often caused bleeding in the **digestive tract.**

4   Then, in the 1800s, a German chemist attempted to reduce these side effects by putting the substance through a series of chemical reactions to change its form. The resulting substance, now known as aspirin, was not only gentler on the stomach—it also did an even better job of relieving pain. People eventually began to call it a "wonder drug."

---

over-the-counter (ō'-vər-<u>th</u>ə-kown'-tər) can be bought at the store without a written order from a doctor
side effects (sīd'-i-fekts') the effects of a drug on the body in addition to how it helps cure the pain or the illness
digestive tract (dī-jes'-tiv-trakt') the series of organs in the body that work together to digest food

The willow trees shown here are the kind used to make aspirin. **Think about how people might have first figured out that willow tree bark eased pain.**

Connect
Use the information in the "Pain Relief from a Plant" section to make a connection. Complete the sentence below.

When I read about how aspirin was invented, it

reminds me _____

_____

_____

because _____

_____

_____

43

Pain Signals Travel to Brain

When you are hurt, the nerves in your body carry pain signals to your brain. Special chemicals called prostaglandins make the pain signals stronger. **Think about how these pain signals help keep your body safe.**

Ouch!

5   To understand why aspirin is effective, first you need to understand how pain works. Although pain is an unpleasant sensation, it's a critical tool for your body. Pain warns you when you're injured so you can protect yourself from further injury. Imagine the things that would happen if you couldn't feel pain. If you accidentally placed your hand on a hot stove, you wouldn't know to take your hand away until you saw that you were badly burned—which could lead to infection, the loss of your limb, or even death.

6   Scientists don't know exactly how we feel pain because the process is extremely complex, but they do know that it involves the nervous system. The body has thousands of nerves that carry messages to and from the brain, much like the way electricity flows through wires. When a part of the body is hurt, the nerves in that spot send a *Damaged!* message to the brain. The brain perceives the message as pain, and it sends a message back to the body to take action: *Remove your hand from the stove right now!*

Find the Main Idea

Reread **paragraph 6**. The main idea of this paragraph is that *the nervous system plays a part in the way we feel pain.*

Is this main idea close to the text or far from the text? Explain your answer.

_____

_____

_____

_____

_____

_____

7   However, at any given moment your brain is processing many different signals from your body. To make sure your brain gets the pain message loud and clear, your body goes one step further. It uses special chemicals called prostaglandins to amplify the pain signal. When a part of your body is damaged, the cells in the area release prostaglandins, which turn up the intensity of the pain signals sent to the brain. This ensures that the *Damaged!* message gets first priority.

Stop the Pain

8   Although pain is a helpful signal at first, ongoing pain can be **debilitating.** That's where aspirin and other pain relievers come in. Aspirin doesn't stop the *cause* of pain—it won't cure a headache or heal a broken arm. Instead, it reduces the intensity of the pain signals sent to the brain by interrupting the production of prostaglandins.

9   Prostaglandins are produced by an **enzyme** called COX-2. Without COX-2, damaged cells can't make prostaglandins. Aspirin attaches to the COX-2 enzyme and acts like a lock, keeping the enzyme from doing its job. Less action from COX-2 means fewer prostaglandins, which means weaker pain messages going to the brain and fewer pain sensations registering in the body.

10   Aspirin also relieves pain in another way. In addition to amplifying pain messages, prostaglandins also trigger inflammation, or swelling, in tissue around damaged cells. By reducing the creation of prostaglandins, aspirin also reduces inflammation. This is how aspirin provides relief for people who suffer from arthritis or other types of **chronic** inflammation of the joints or tissues.

11   Aspirin has many positive effects but, as with any other over-the-counter drug, you should be aware of its possible negative side effects.

---

enzyme (en'-zīm') a chemical substance made by plants and animals that helps changes happen inside them

Think about how aspirin works in the body to relieve a headache.

Find the Main Idea

Reread **paragraph 9.** Study the details to determine what they have in common. Then infer the main idea of the paragraph. Write the main idea below.

_____

_____

_____

_____

A Word of Caution

12   Even though today's aspirin is gentler than the substance from the willow tree bark used long ago, it can still harm the stomach. Why? Once again, the answer relates to prostaglandins.

Find the Main Idea

Reread **paragraph 13**. Infer the main idea of the paragraph. Write the main idea below.

_____

_____

_____

_____

How did you determine the main idea?

_____

_____

_____

_____

13   Prostaglandins serve another important function in the body: they help maintain the thick lining inside your stomach. This lining protects the wall of the stomach from the strong acids your body produces to help digest food. Because aspirin reduces prostaglandins, repeated doses of aspirin can cause the stomach lining to become too thin. The digestive acids then begin to irritate the stomach wall. This sometimes leads to sores or even bleeding in the stomach.

14   Another important thing to know about aspirin is that it can be dangerous for children. Doctors have noticed a **correlation** between children who take aspirin and those who develop a rare disease called Reye's syndrome. This disease attacks body organs, including the liver and the brain, and can be fatal. Although it has not been proven that aspirin causes Reye's syndrome, most doctors do not recommend aspirin for children under the age of 16.

Other Options

15   The risks and negative side effects of taking aspirin prompted doctors and scientists to create substitutes for aspirin. One aspirin substitute is made from a substance called acetaminophen.

16   Acetaminophen was first sold in 1960 as an over-the-counter pain reliever specifically for children. Although acetaminophen blocks prostaglandins, like aspirin does, it blocks them in the brain instead of at the source of the pain. So, unlike aspirin, acetaminophen does not reduce inflammation in the body.

17   In 1984 another aspirin substitute, made from a substance called ibuprofen, hit the over-the-counter market. Like aspirin, ibuprofen stops both pain *and* swelling. Both of these aspirin substitutes are considered safe for children.

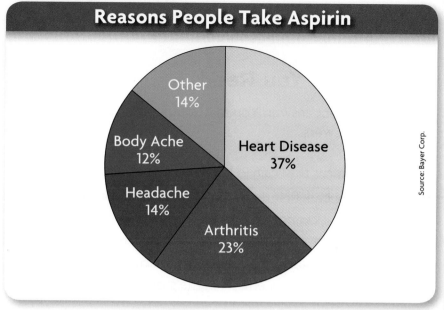

Reasons People Take Aspirin

Other 14%

Body Ache 12%

Heart Disease 37%

Headache 14%

Arthritis 23%

Source: Bayer Corp.

This pie chart shows that heart disease is the most common reason people take aspirin. Arthritis is the second most common reason. **Think about how aspirin helps relieve both pain and swelling caused by arthritis.**

18   Despite the alternatives, many adults continue to take aspirin. In fact, as a group, adults in the United States consume about 80 million aspirin tablets per day. But many adults who take aspirin do not take it for pain relief; rather, they take it to protect their hearts.

From the Heart

19   Recently, doctors have learned that aspirin can help prevent heart attacks by making blood clots less likely to form. Your blood clots in order to stop the loss of blood when you have an injury such as a bloody nose or a cut. But occasionally a blood clot mistakenly forms inside the blood vessels. If this happens, the clot can travel through the body and eventually get stuck in the vessels leading to the heart. This can cause a heart attack. So some older adults—and many adults who have had heart surgery—take a low daily dose of aspirin to help prevent heart attacks.

20   The next time you see someone reaching for an aspirin, think about how this little pill, smaller than a dime, works its wonders in the body.

Connect

Use the information in **paragraph 19** to make a connection. Complete the sentence below.

When I read about _____

_____

_____

it reminds me _____

_____

_____

because _____

_____

_____

Self-Check

Look back at the prediction you wrote on page 42.

• Does your prediction match the text? Why or why not?

Write your answers on a separate sheet of paper.

Understanding What You Read

Fill in the circle next to the correct answer. You may look back at the text to help you choose the correct answers.

1. Which of these **best** summarizes the "Pain Relief from a Plant" section?
    - ○ A. A substance in willow bark first relieved pain thousands of years ago, and later a chemist changed it into the gentler form now known as aspirin.
    - ○ B. The pain-relieving substance in the bark of the willow tree relieved pain, but it also caused bad side effects in the stomach and digestive tract.
    - ○ C. A chemist created aspirin by putting a substance through a series of chemical reactions that made it better at relieving pain and gentler on the stomach.

2. When a part of the body is hurt,
    - ○ A. the nerves in that spot send a *Damaged!* message to the brain.
    - ○ B. the result is usually serious infection or even death.
    - ○ C. the body tells the brain to take action.

3. Which of these is an effect of Reye's syndrome?
    - ○ A. blood clots
    - ○ B. stomach sores
    - ○ C. liver problems

4. Which of these does **not** reduce swelling?
    - ○ A. aspirin
    - ○ B. ibuprofen
    - ○ C. acetaminophen

5. The pie chart titled "Reasons People Take Aspirin" helps support the author's point that adults
    - ○ A. take aspirin more often than children do.
    - ○ B. often take aspirin to protect their hearts.
    - ○ C. take about 80 million aspirin tablets per day.

Score 4 points for each correct answer.

_____ /20 **Total Score: Activity A**

Finding the Main Idea and Details

Paragraph 10 from the article is shown below. Read the paragraph. Then use the paragraph to complete the activities.

Aspirin also relieves pain in another way. In addition to amplifying pain messages, prostaglandins also trigger inflammation, or swelling, in tissue around damaged cells. By reducing the creation of prostaglandins, aspirin also reduces inflammation. This is how aspirin provides relief for people who suffer from arthritis or other types of chronic inflammation of the joints or tissues.

1. Look for details in the paragraph that have something in common. Write **three** of these details on the lines below.

Detail _____

Detail _____

Detail _____

2. Use the details you wrote to infer the main idea. Write the main idea below. Then explain how you determined this to be the main idea.

Main Idea _____

_____

Explanation _____

_____

_____

_____

Score 5 points each for numbers 1 and 2.

_____ /10 **Total Score: Activity B**

Using Words

Follow the instructions below. Write your answers on the lines.

1. List **two** things that are often **extracted** from foods.

    _____

    _____

2. List **three** things that can be **ingested** by people.

    _____

    _____

    _____

3. List **two** things that could have a **debilitating** effect on you.

    _____

    _____

4. List **two** issues that are **chronic** problems in the world.

    _____

    _____

5. List **two** examples of the **correlation** between the way you think and the way you feel.

    _____

    _____

Score 4 points for each correct answer.

_____ /20   **Total Score: Activity C**

Writing About It

Write a Poster Suppose you work in a doctor's office. Write a poster to educate patients about aspirin. Finish the sentences below to write your poster. Be sure your writing matches the information in the text. Use the checklist on page 119 to check your work.

Learn More About Aspirin

◆ Aspirin blocks pain by _____
_____
_____

◆ For people who are at risk for heart attacks,
_____
_____

◆ Aspirin is not for everyone because _____
_____
_____

◆ Doctors do not recommend aspirin _____
_____
_____

Lesson 4 Add your scores from activities A, B, and C to get your total score.

_____ **A** Understanding What You Read
_____ **B** Finding the Main Idea and Details
_____ **C** Using Words
_____ **Total Score**

Multiply your **Total Score x 2** _____
This is your percentage score.
Record your percentage score on the graph on page 121.

INFECTIOUS DISEASES
Bugs You Don't Want to Catch

Infectious (in-fek'-shəs) diseases
are caused by tiny germs like the
ones shown here, which were
photographed under a microscope.

READING SKILL ## Taking Notes

One way to understand and remember what you read is to take two-column notes. To **take notes** this way, readers divide a piece of paper into two columns. In the narrower left column, they write the main ideas and topics from the text. Then, in the wider right column, they write the details related to each main idea or topic. Good note takers keep their notes brief by using short, precise phrases. Taking two-column notes can help you organize your thoughts about the information in the text. It can also help you study for tests.

EXAMPLE

> In 1793 a disease called yellow fever swept through the city of Philadelphia. The disease spread from person to person through the bites of mosquitoes. It caused horrible symptoms that eventually ended in death. It is believed that about 5,000 people died from yellow fever that year. More than half the population fled the city to avoid catching the disease.

Here is what two-column notes might look like for the example paragraph above. The topic of the paragraph is written on the left side, and the details are written on the right. Notice how all the notes are short and precise.

1793 yellow fever disease in Philadelphia	– spread through mosquito bites – caused horrible symptoms – killed 5,000 people – half the population fled

Get ready to take two-column notes as you read about infectious diseases.

1. First get **two** blank sheets of paper. Then draw a line from the top to the bottom of each page. Make the left column narrower than the right column.

2. As you read, write the main ideas and topics in the left column. Write details and definitions in the right column. Make sure to take notes on **at least two** main ideas or topics for each page of text.

Getting Ready to Read

Think About What You Know

CONNECT Think about the last time you were sick. What caused your illness? What do you know about how diseases spread from one person to another? Write your answers here.

_____

_____

_____

Word Power

PREVIEW Read the words and definitions below. Then look ahead at the title and at the headings and images in the article.

tainted (tānt'-əd)	touched or affected by something harmful
immunity (i-mū'-nə-tē)	the ability of a living thing to resist disease
outbreaks (owt'-brāks')	sudden increases in the number of people experiencing a disease
mutate (mū'-tāt')	to change in form or structure
eradicate (i-ra'-də-kāt')	to completely stop or eliminate something

QUESTION Use the words, title, headings, and images to ask a question. What would you like to know about infectious diseases? Write your question on the lines below.

_____

_____

_____

Reason to Read

Read to find out if the information in the text answers your question. At the end of the article, you will be asked to look back at your question. You will decide whether or not your question is answered in the text.

INFECTIOUS DISEASES
Bugs You Don't Want to Catch

1   Have you ever arrived at school on a winter morning to discover that many of your classmates are absent? Later you hear that the flu is going around school—and you might start to wonder if you'll be the next one to catch it.

Different Kinds of Germs

2   Flus and colds are examples of infectious diseases, which are illnesses caused by **microscopic** things known as germs that get into the body and multiply. Two types of germs that can cause infectious diseases are bacteria and viruses.

3   Bacteria are one-celled organisms that thrive in a variety of environments, including the human body. Most bacteria are harmless; some are actually helpful. Helpful bacteria include several species of *Lactobacillus* that live in your intestines and help keep you healthy. Some bacteria, however, cause disease by invading and damaging tissues inside the body. *Streptococcus*, which causes strep throat, is an example of a disease-causing bacterium. (*Bacterium* is the singular form of *bacteria*.)

4   Viruses are even tinier than bacteria. Unlike bacteria, viruses can't reproduce on their own. They must invade living cells and use them as hosts in order to reproduce; this eventually kills the cells, causing illness. Flus and colds are examples of diseases caused by viruses.

Take Notes

Remember to take notes as you read. Write the main ideas and topics in the left column. Write details and definitions in the right column.

- Take notes on **at least two** main ideas or topics for each page of text.
- Use the headings to help you find the main ideas or topics.

---

microscopic (mī′-krə-skä′-pik) so small that you can't see it without a special lens or microscope

Take Notes

Use your paper to take notes about the information on this page.

- Remember to put the main ideas and topics in the left column and the details and definitions in the right column.
- Remember to use short, precise phrases.

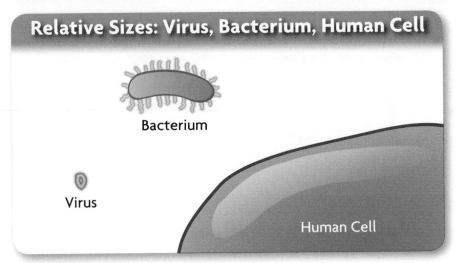

Relative Sizes: Virus, Bacterium, Human Cell

Bacterium

Virus

Human Cell

This drawing shows how the sizes of a virus and a bacterium relate to each other and to the size of a human cell. You can see that the virus is much smaller than both the bacterium and the human cell. **Think about the ways germs' tiny size allows them to spread easily from person to person.**

Keep It to Yourself

5   Bacteria and viruses get transmitted, or passed on, to people in a variety of ways. Some diseases are contagious, which means they can pass easily from person to person through direct or indirect contact. For example, someone with a cold can spread it to people by coughing or sneezing around them or by touching something that other people touch, such as a doorknob. Diseases that spread this way are difficult to contain because people interact constantly at work, at school, on the bus, and in the grocery store. But you can do your part to contain contagious diseases by covering your mouth when you cough and by washing your hands regularly—especially when you have a cold or flu.

6   Some contagious diseases, such as hepatitis or AIDS, spread only through the direct transfer of bodily fluids such as blood. Most diseases that transmit this way are caused by viruses.

Find the Source

People in many parts of the world do not have access to clean water. They must use unfiltered water from rivers or lakes for drinking and bathing. In these areas, infectious diseases are very hard to control. **Think about where your drinking water comes from.**

7   Some diseases are not contagious between people; rather, people catch them from a common source such as contaminated drinking water or food. For example, food poisoning made national headlines in 2006–2007 when hundreds of people across 39 states became ill from eating peanut butter **tainted** with *Salmonella* bacteria.

8   Some diseases spread by way of a carrier, such as an insect that bites. Malaria, which is transmitted to people through certain mosquitoes, is one example of this kind of disease.

Your Defenses

9   If all this talk about catching diseases is making you nervous, remember this: if you come into contact with harmful germs, it doesn't necessarily mean you will get sick. This is because your body can defend itself from many infectious diseases by building up **immunity** to them. You develop immunity when your body creates antibodies, which are special proteins that attack foreign particles that enter the body. But it takes time for your body to build immunity to different diseases.

10   The first time it encounters a particular disease-causing germ, your body goes to work to produce antibodies against the germ. The germ might make you ill, but when you build up enough antibodies to recover, those antibodies remain in your system. So the next time you come into contact with that germ, your body is ready to fight it off before you get sick. This explains why you get sick only once from certain diseases, such as chicken pox. (To learn more about antibodies, read the allergies article in *World Works, Level E,* Lesson 7.)

Powerful Medicine

11   For times when your body gets caught without enough immunity to something, there are medicines available called antibiotics. If you've ever suffered from a sore throat or an ear infection, you may have taken antibiotics to get rid of the infection. But remember the difference in how bacteria and viruses reproduce? While antibiotics do a great job destroying bacterial infections, they don't work against viruses. Viruses reproduce and cause disease by getting inside your cells, so destroying the virus would mean destroying the cells. However, scientists have created some medicines that can slow and even halt the reproduction of certain viruses.

Take Notes

Use your paper to take notes about the information on this page. Remember to take notes on **at least two** main ideas or topics.

Connect

Use the information in the "Your Defenses" section to make a connection. Complete the sentence below.

When I read about _____

_____

_____

it reminds me _____

_____

_____

because _____

_____

_____

12   Another method scientists use to combat the spread of bacteria and viruses is something you may already be familiar with: vaccines. Vaccines help your body build immunity by introducing a weakened or dead sample of a type of bacteria or virus into your body orally or through injection. The sample in the vaccine is too weak to make you sick, but it's enough to prompt your immune system to make antibodies against the germ. If you ever come into contact with that virus or bacterium out in the world, the antibodies you need are already there, ready to spring into action and destroy the germs.

13   Unfortunately, despite the efforts of modern medicine, large and often devastating **outbreaks** of disease still occur.

Widespread Disease

14   When many people contract a disease in a single town or country, the outbreak is called an epidemic. When an epidemic affects an excessive amount of people or spreads to numerous countries around the world, it is called a pandemic.

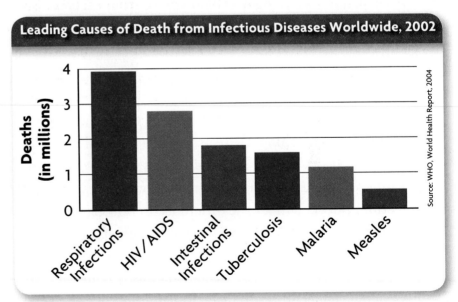

Leading Causes of Death from Infectious Diseases Worldwide, 2002

Deaths (in millions)

Respiratory Infections · HIV/AIDS · Intestinal Infections · Tuberculosis · Malaria · Measles

Source: WHO, World Health Report, 2004

HIV/AIDS, one of the most deadly infectious diseases in the world today, is considered a pandemic. **Think about whether there are any diseases on this bar graph that you have never heard of. Look up these diseases in a dictionary or on the Internet.**

15   A pandemic can occur when a type of virus or bacteria is introduced into a population that has not encountered it before. Because the population has not built up any immunity against it, the new germ will be able to infect the people with full force.

16   One way people can get caught without immunity is when animal viruses **mutate** and become able to infect humans. This happened in 1918 when a flu virus that usually infected birds mutated, infected humans, and then began to pass from person to person. The resulting disease, called Spanish flu, killed between 25 and 50 million people worldwide.

What About Now?

17   Modern transportation allows people to travel across the world in a matter of hours, making it possible for disease to spread from country to country more quickly than ever before. At international airports, thousands of people from countries all over the world cross paths every day in restrooms, waiting areas, and restaurants. Health care authorities are very aware of this risk. Recently disease experts have been closely monitoring the **avian flu** virus, which has the potential to mutate and pass between humans. A few people have caught avian flu by coming into contact with infected birds. However, as long as the virus is not contagious between people, it will be unable to spread.

18   While there is still a long way to go to **eradicate** all infectious diseases, scientists have succeeded in controlling many previously common diseases, such as **polio** and **smallpox,** through vaccines and medicine. Hopefully, over time, more and more infectious diseases will become less and less common.

---

avian flu (āʹ-vē-ən-flo͞oʹ) a type of deadly flu virus that infects birds and can sometimes spread to humans
polio (pōʹ-lē-ōʹ) a highly contagious disease, caused by a virus, that usually occurs in children and can cause weakened muscles or the inability to move certain body parts
smallpox (smôlʹ-päksʹ) a highly contagious disease, caused by a virus, that has symptoms including fever, weakness, and blisterlike sores on the skin

During an outbreak of a disease called SARS in 2003, people had to be very careful when traveling between countries. **Think about how wearing masks would help keep some diseases from spreading.**

Take Notes
Use your paper to take notes about the information on this page. When you are finished reading the article, review your notes.

Self-Check
Look back at the question you wrote on page 54.
• Does the information in the text answer your question? If it does, what is the answer? If it does not, where could you look to find more information?
Write your answers on a separate sheet of paper.

Understanding What You Read

Fill in the circle next to the correct answer. You may look back at the text to help you choose the correct answers.

1. Viruses are different from bacteria because only viruses can
   - ○ A. cause infectious diseases.
   - ○ B. help you digest your food.
   - ○ C. take over cells in the body.

2. How does washing your hands regularly help solve the problem of infectious diseases?
   - ○ A. It can reduce the spread of germs.
   - ○ B. It stops the transfer of bodily fluids.
   - ○ C. It protects you from bacteria in food.

3. The first time it encounters a particular disease-causing germ, your body
   - ○ A. lets that germ infect only a small area.
   - ○ B. goes to work to produce antibodies against the germ.
   - ○ C. rarely gets the disease because it's already immune to the germ.

4. The bar graph titled "Leading Causes of Death from Infectious Diseases Worldwide, 2002" helps support the author's point that
   - ○ A. antibiotics do a great job of fighting bacteria.
   - ○ B. lack of immunity causes diseases to spread quickly.
   - ○ C. there is still a long way to go to stop infectious diseases.

5. From the information in the "What About Now?" section, you can infer that
   - ○ A. avian flu has the potential to be a serious threat to world health.
   - ○ B. modern transportation will solve the problem of infectious diseases.
   - ○ C. health care authorities don't think vaccines can help improve health.

Score 4 points for each correct answer.
_____/20   **Total Score: Activity A**

Taking Notes

Paragraph 5 from the article is shown below. Read the paragraph. Then use the paragraph to complete the activities.

Bacteria and viruses get transmitted, or passed on, to people in a variety of ways. Some diseases are contagious, which means they can pass easily from person to person through direct or indirect contact. For example, someone with a cold can spread it to people by coughing or sneezing around them or by touching something that other people touch, such as a doorknob. Diseases that spread this way are difficult to contain because people interact constantly at work, at school, on the bus, and in the grocery store. But you can do your part to contain contagious diseases by covering your mouth when you cough and by washing your hands regularly—especially when you have a cold or flu.

1. Fill in the circle next to the phrase that **best** states the topic of the paragraph.
   - ○ A. how contagious diseases spread
   - ○ B. why you should wash your hands
   - ○ C. learning about bacteria and viruses

2. Use the notebook page below to show how you would take notes on the paragraph. Write the paragraph topic and **at least three** details.

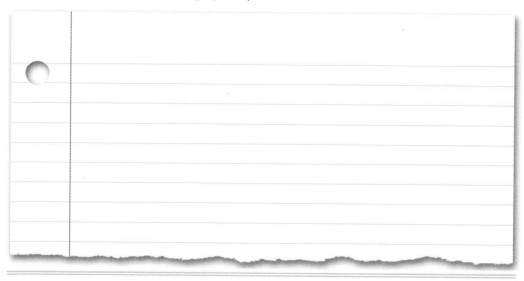

Score 5 points each for numbers 1 and 2.

_____ /10   **Total Score: Activity B**

Using Words

Complete the analogies below by writing a word from the box on each line.
Remember that in an analogy, the last two words must be related in the same
way that the first two are related.

> **tainted**   **immunity**   **outbreaks**
> **mutate**   **eradicate**

1. smile : grin : : change : _____

2. rain : storms : : disease : _____

3. true : false : : pure : _____

4. give : take : : spread : _____

5. home : apartment : : protection : _____

Choose one word from the box. Write a sentence using the word. Be sure
to put at least one detail in your sentence. The detail should show that you
understand what the word means.

6. _____

_____

Score 4 points for each correct answer in numbers 1–5.
(Do not score number 6.)
_____ /20   **Total Score: Activity C**

Writing About It

Write a Comic Strip Write a comic strip about a cold that spreads between two friends. Finish the sentences in each bubble to write your comic strip. Be sure your writing matches the information in the text. Use the checklist on page 119 to check your work.

Lesson 5 Add your scores from activities A, B, and C to get your total score.

_____ **A** Understanding What You Read

_____ **B** Taking Notes

_____ **C** Using Words

_____ **Total Score**

Multiply your **Total Score x 2** _____

This is your percentage score.

Record your percentage score on the graph on page 121.

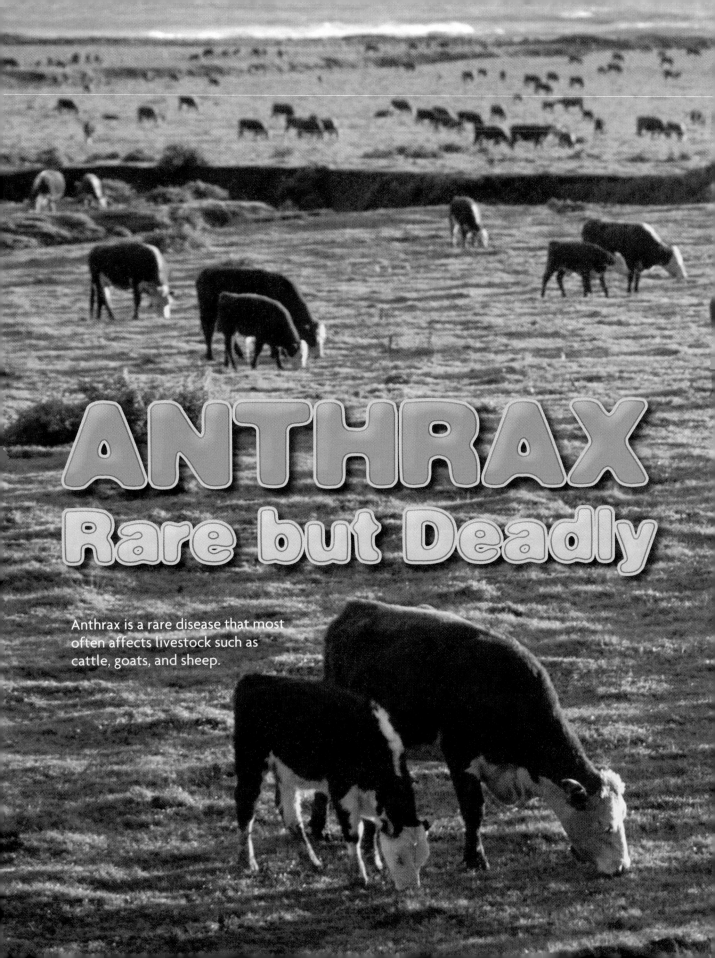

ANTHRAX
Rare but Deadly

Anthrax is a rare disease that most often affects livestock such as cattle, goats, and sheep.

READING SKILL | Summarizing

A **summary** is a shortened version of a text that includes key words from the text as well as your own words. A summary includes only the most important ideas from the text. When you read, look for key words and phrases that explain *who, what, when, where, why,* and *how.* These key words will help you find the most important ideas. A summary should be about 20 words or less and should be easy for someone to understand.

EXAMPLE

The U.S. Postal Service handles billions of pieces of mail each year. In addition to delivering mail on time, postal workers must inspect the mail to make sure it's safe. Although it happens very rarely, people sometimes try to send harmful materials—even bombs—through the mail.

Postal service employees isolate and investigate letters and packages that look suspicious. These might include items that have extra tape, no return address, or unusual stains. Workers can use X-ray machines or certain procedures to check an item further. Most of these items turn out to be harmless.

Here is what a summary diagram might look like for the example paragraphs above. The most important ideas are shown in the top boxes. The summary belongs in the bottom box. Use the most important ideas to write a summary of the example paragraphs.

> People sometimes try to send harmful materials through the mail.

> Postal workers investigate mail that looks suspicious.

Getting Ready to Read

Think About What You Know

CONNECT Think about the things people use as weapons. Why do you think people might try to use germs, such as bacteria, as weapons? Write your answer here.

_____

_____

_____

Word Power

PREVIEW Read the words and definitions below. Then look ahead at the title and at the headings and images in the article.

obscure (əb-skyoor′)	not well known
resistant (ri-zis′-tənt)	able to remain unharmed or unaffected by something
revert (ri-vərt′)	to go back to a previous form or way of being
activate (ak′-tə-vāt′)	to cause a process to begin working
lethal (lē′-thəl)	able to cause death

PREDICT Use the words, title, headings, and images to make a prediction. What do you think the author will say about anthrax?

I predict the author will _____

_____

because _____

_____

Reason to Read

Read to find out if the prediction you wrote above matches the information in the text. At the end of the article, you will be asked about your prediction. You will need to explain how your prediction is the same as the text or different from it.

ANTHRAX
Rare but Deadly

1   Although it has been around for thousands of years, anthrax was unknown to most Americans until a few years ago. That's because few people in the United States had ever caught this deadly disease. That changed in 2001 when someone purposely put anthrax into letters and sent them through the U.S. mail. Twenty-two people got sick, and five of them died. Anthrax was no longer just an **obscure** disease—it was a potential weapon.

Anthrax and Animals

2   Anthrax is caused by a kind of bacteria. For much of their lifetime the bacteria exist as spores, or tiny dormant bodies that come to life only under certain environmental conditions. Anthrax spores are odorless, colorless, and tasteless and can be smaller than specks of dust. They live in soil, have tough outer casings that are highly **resistant** to the effects of sunlight, and can withstand extreme temperatures and lack of water. Because they are exceptionally hardy, the spores can survive for decades.

3   Under certain environmental conditions, the spores germinate, or grow, into bacteria. The bacteria thrive as long as these favorable conditions last. If conditions change, the bacteria **revert** to spores and become dormant again.

4   What environmental conditions are needed to trigger the germination of anthrax spores? Anthrax bacteria are perfectly suited to grow in the intestines of some types of animals, where warmth, moisture, and certain chemical compounds can **activate** the spores. That's great for the bacteria but not for the animal. As the bacteria grow, they produce toxins, or poisons, that damage or kill cells and can inhibit the body's natural defenses. The toxins are so **lethal** that acute cases of anthrax can kill an animal within 24 hours.

Think about why more animals might get anthrax during a drought when the grass is very short.

Summarize

Reread **paragraph 2**. Find the important ideas by looking for key words and phrases that answer the questions *who, what, when, where, why,* and *how.* Write the key words and phrases here.

_____

_____

_____

_____

Use the key words and phrases to write a summary of the paragraph.

_____

_____

_____

_____

_____

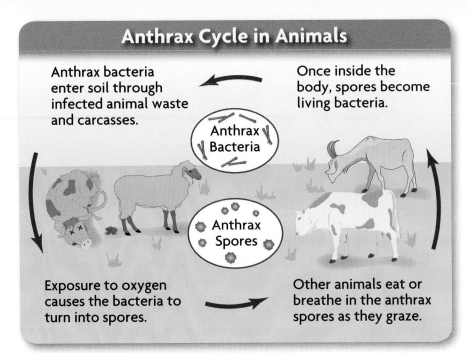

Anthrax Cycle in Animals

Anthrax bacteria enter soil through infected animal waste and carcasses.

Once inside the body, spores become living bacteria.

Anthrax Bacteria

Anthrax Spores

Exposure to oxygen causes the bacteria to turn into spores.

Other animals eat or breathe in the anthrax spores as they graze.

This diagram shows the role that animals play in the anthrax cycle. **Think about one thing people could do to help break this cycle.**

Summarize

Not all ideas in a text are important enough to be included in a summary. Reread **paragraph 5**. Write one idea you would **not** include in a summary of this paragraph.

_____

_____

_____

Now find the most important ideas and use them to write a summary of this paragraph.

_____

_____

_____

_____

_____

_____

Reread your summary. Look for any unimportant details that should not be included. Then rewrite your summary on a separate sheet of paper if needed.

5   Anthrax bacteria most commonly infect grass-eating animals such as cows, goats, and sheep. The disease does not spread from one animal to another. Rather, an animal must come into direct contact with the spores—usually by eating them. As the animals graze, they bite off bits of anthrax-infected soil along with the grass. Animals can also get anthrax by inhaling dust that contains the spores.

The Human Factor

6   Although it happens rarely, humans can also get anthrax. There are three ways this can happen. Cutaneous anthrax, or skin anthrax, occurs when spores or bacteria enter the body through a cut or open sore on the skin. This is a danger for workers who handle the meat, wool, or hides of infected animals. However, an anthrax **vaccine** has been available for animals since the 1880s. The livestock vaccination programs of many countries are so good that only a small number of animals each year get the disease. Vaccinating livestock has helped prevent people from getting cutaneous anthrax from animals.

vaccine (vak-sēn′) a weak or dead sample of a disease-causing germ that is used to help protect people or animals against the disease

7   Intestinal anthrax occurs when someone eats undercooked meat from an animal infected with anthrax spores. This is even rarer than cutaneous anthrax due to strict safety regulations in meat processing plants. In fact, in the United States there has never been a confirmed case of intestinal anthrax.

8   The rarest form, inhalation anthrax, occurs when spores get into the air, a person inhales them, and they enter the lungs. Both inhalation and cutaneous anthrax caused problems in 2001. Anthrax spores were mixed into a powder, sprinkled on letters, and mailed to television stations and newspaper offices in New York and Florida and to two U.S. senators in Washington, D.C. Several people at these locations were exposed to the spores, as were postal workers and hospital workers. Although police traced the letters back to a city mailbox in New Jersey, no arrests were ever made.

Signs and Symptoms

9   What happens when a person gets anthrax? The symptoms differ depending on the form of anthrax, but they are all very unpleasant. Cutaneous anthrax causes swelling and sores with black centers on the skin within as little as one to two days of exposure. Intestinal anthrax causes **diarrhea,** fever, and stomach pain soon after contaminated meat is eaten. Inhalation anthrax initially causes flulike symptoms that, after several days, progress to **shock** and lung failure. Without proper treatment, all forms of anthrax can ultimately cause death.

Fighting Back

10   Anthrax is a serious disease, but medical treatments are available for it. Because anthrax is caused by bacteria, antibiotic medicines that kill the bacteria can get rid of it. If they are administered quickly, the antibiotics can save a person's life.

---

diarrhea (dī′-ə-rē′-ə) a condition in which the waste from a person's bowels is watery and needs to be released frequently
shock (shäk) a life-threatening condition in which the body fails to supply enough blood and oxygen to the cells

69

Summarize

Sometimes you may be asked to summarize more than one paragraph at a time. Reread **paragraphs 11** and **12**. Write down the most important idea in each paragraph.

1. _____

_____

2. _____

_____

Now use these ideas to write a summary of the two paragraphs. Remember that your summary should be about 20 words or less.

_____

_____

_____

_____

_____

_____

11   Unfortunately, if anthrax isn't caught and treated early on, the toxins released by the bacteria can increase to deadly levels. Cutaneous anthrax is usually caught early because the symptoms are easy to identify. Inhalation anthrax, however, is tougher to treat because most symptoms don't appear until the bacteria and toxins have already spread throughout a person's body and caused irreversible tissue damage. As a result, the death rate for inhalation anthrax is very high.

12   Although it's good to be aware of the symptoms of anthrax, it's also important to remember that this disease is very rare. The average person's risk of exposure to anthrax spores is very, very low. However, there is some concern that anthrax spores might be used as a weapon again someday.

Anthrax as a Weapon

13   As the 2001 anthrax scare unfolded, some people were worried that terrorists could get anthrax spores from a research laboratory, cultivate them, and then spray them over a large city.

During the anthrax scare in 2001, investigators had to wear protective suits and breathe through special masks to avoid possible contact with the spores. **Think about what would have to be done to clean up infected areas before people could safely enter them.**

14   Fortunately, spreading anthrax is not that easy. People trying to grow large numbers of anthrax spores would run the risk of first accidentally contaminating themselves and others nearby. This actually happened in 1979, in the former Soviet Union, when military scientists were experimenting with **biological weapons.** Anthrax spores leaked out of their laboratory and killed 66 people.

15   Many scientists also believe that spreading anthrax powder over a large city with any accuracy would be difficult due to unpredictable variations in wind speed and direction. Therefore, many experts say that anthrax would never be used as a weapon of mass destruction.

16   Still, it has been demonstrated that anthrax spores can be used in smaller amounts to target a few people and create a general sense of panic. For this reason, government agencies are currently building up their supplies of anthrax antibiotics, and scientists are working on developing new anthrax vaccines for humans.

17   Although anthrax is a scary prospect, reading this article is probably as close as you will ever get to experiencing anthrax.

Did You Know?

A human vaccine against anthrax does exist today. However, most of the people who receive it are either anthrax researchers or military personnel whose missions might put them at risk for exposure. The vaccination process involves multiple doses and can cause negative side effects, or symptoms. This is why scientists are working to create new vaccines.

---

biological weapons (bī-ə-lä′-ji-kəl-we′-pənz) weapons of war that expose people to disease-causing germs or poisonous substances

Connect
Use the information in **paragraph 14** to make a connection. Complete the sentence below.

When I read about _____

_____

_____

it reminds me _____

_____

because _____

_____

_____

Self-Check
Look back at the prediction you wrote on page 66.
• Does your prediction match the text? Why or why not?
Write your answers on a separate sheet of paper.

Understanding What You Read

Fill in the circle next to the correct answer. You may look back at the text to help you choose the correct answers.

1. Which sentence **best** states the main idea in paragraph 1?
   - ○ A. Anthrax has been around for thousands of years.
   - ○ B. In 2001 Americans became more aware of anthrax.
   - ○ C. Five people died from anthrax sent through the U.S. mail.

2. From the diagram titled "Anthrax Cycle in Animals," what must happen **before** anthrax bacteria will turn into spores?
   - ○ A. The bacteria must be exposed to oxygen.
   - ○ B. The bacteria must be taken from the soil.
   - ○ C. The bacteria must enter an animal's body.

3. Cutaneous anthrax causes
   - ○ A. flulike symptoms.
   - ○ B. diarrhea, fever, and stomach pain.
   - ○ C. swelling and sores with black centers on the skin.

4. What is the cause of the high death rate associated with inhalation anthrax?
   - ○ A. Symptoms appear after the bacteria has spread, so treatment often begins too late.
   - ○ B. The spores spread through the lungs, making it hard for the body to get oxygen.
   - ○ C. Antibiotics don't have the same effect when the anthrax has been inhaled.

5. The author included the "Did You Know?" box on page 71 to
   - ○ A. restate the most important ideas in the article.
   - ○ B. explain his or her opinion of the anthrax vaccines.
   - ○ C. provide more details about one of the ideas in the text.

Score 4 points for each correct answer.
_____/20 **Total Score: Activity A**

72

Summarizing

Paragraphs 14 and 15 from the article are shown below. Read the paragraphs. Then use the paragraphs to complete the activities.

Fortunately, spreading anthrax is not that easy. People trying to grow large numbers of anthrax spores would run the risk of first accidentally contaminating themselves and others nearby. This actually happened in 1979, in the former Soviet Union, when military scientists were experimenting with biological weapons. Anthrax spores leaked out of their laboratory and killed 66 people.

Many scientists also believe that spreading anthrax powder over a large city with any accuracy would be difficult due to unpredictable variations in wind speed and direction. Therefore, many experts say that anthrax would never be used as a weapon of mass destruction.

1. Fill in the circle next to the idea that is **not** important enough to be included in a summary of the paragraphs above.

    ○ A. Spreading anthrax over a city would be difficult.
    ○ B. A leak of anthrax spores once killed 66 people.
    ○ C. People who grow spores risk catching anthrax.

2. Write the **three** most important ideas from the paragraphs above in the top boxes of the summary diagram below. Then write your summary in the bottom box. Make sure your summary is about 20 words or less.

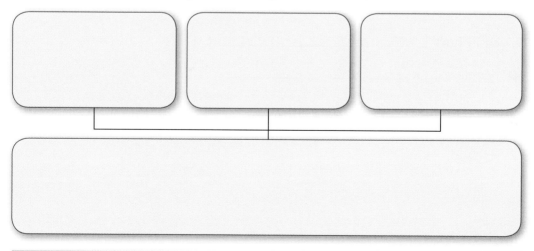

Score 5 points each for numbers 1 and 2.

_____ /10   **Total Score: Activity B**

Using Words

The words and phrases in the list below relate to the words in the box. Some words or phrases in the list are synonyms. They have the same meaning. Some words or phrases are antonyms. They have the opposite meaning. Write the related word from the box on each line. Use each word from the box **twice.**

obscure	resistant	revert
activate	lethal	

Synonyms

1. trigger _____

2. deadly _____

3. return _____

4. not affected _____

5. rare _____

Antonyms

6. stay the same _____

7. famous _____

8. turn off _____

9. easily hurt _____

10. harmless _____

Score 2 points for each correct answer.

_____ /20   **Total Score: Activity C**

Writing About It

Write a Magazine Article Suppose you work for a newsmagazine. Write an article about anthrax. The purpose of your article is to state the facts clearly, without exaggeration or drama. Finish the sentences below to write your article. Be sure your writing matches the information in the text. Use the checklist on page 119 to check your work.

Anthrax is a disease that _____

_____

_____

Anthrax is caused by _____

_____

Anthrax tends not to affect many people because _____

_____

_____

However, there was an anthrax scare in 2001 when _____

_____

_____

It is unlikely that anthrax could be used as a weapon of mass

destruction because _____

_____

_____

Lesson 6 Add your scores from activities A, B, and C to get your total score.

_____ **A** Understanding What You Read
_____ **B** Summarizing
_____ **C** Using Words
_____ **Total Score**

Multiply your **Total Score x 2** _____
This is your percentage score.
Record your percentage score on the graph on page 121.

Compare and Contrast

You read three articles about health in Unit Two. Think about the topic of each article. Then choose **two** of the articles. Write the titles of the articles in the chart below. In the left and right columns, write the ways that the two topics are different. In the center column, write the ways that they are similar.

Title _____	Similarities	Title _____

Use the chart above to write a summary of how these health topics are alike and different. Finish the sentences below to write your summary.

_____ and _____ are different

because _____

_____

_____ and _____ are similar

because _____

_____

Unit 3
Everyday Things

Hybrid Cars

Plastic

Landfills

Plastic
Part of Everyday Life

Plastic comes in many shapes and sizes and is used in thousands of ways every day.

READING SKILL **Reviewing the Reading Skills**

You practiced three reading skills in Unit One. Rate your understanding of each skill using the chart below. Use the following rating scale:

3 I understand this skill well. I use it easily and correctly while I read.

2 I understand this skill a little bit. I sometimes use it correctly while I read.

1 I don't understand this skill. I am not able to use it while I read.

Mark the box under the number 3, 2, or 1 for each skill.

	3	2	1	Need to review?		Turn to:
Making Connections				Yes	No	Lesson 1, page 3
Asking Questions				Yes	No	Lesson 2, page 15
Visualizing				Yes	No	Lesson 3, page 27

If you rated your understanding of a skill at 2 or 1, look back at the lesson page where that skill was taught. The lesson page is shown in the chart above. Reread the skill definition and the example. This will help you get ready to complete the next lesson.

After you have reviewed the skills, complete the sentences below.

The skill I find most helpful when reading is _____

because _____

_____

During this lesson, one thing I can do to improve my reading is _____

_____

_____

Getting Ready to Read

Think About What You Know

CONNECT Look around you. What do you see that is made out of plastic? What do you know about where plastic comes from? Write your answers here.

_____

_____

_____

Word Power

PREVIEW Read the words and definitions below. Then look ahead at the title and at the headings and images in the article.

durable (door'-ə-bəl)	able to stay in good shape even if used a lot
versatile (vər'-sə-təl)	having a large variety of uses
adverse (ad'-vərs')	harmful or not helpful
downside (down'-sīd')	a negative aspect of something
disposable (di-spō'-zə-bəl)	made to be thrown away after being used once or only a few times

QUESTION Use the words, title, headings, and images to ask a question. What would you like to know about plastic? Write your question on the lines below.

_____

_____

_____

Reason to Read

Read to find out if the information in the text answers your question. At the end of the article, you will be asked to look back at your question. You will decide whether or not your question is answered in the text.

Plastic
Part of Everyday Life

Believe it or not, some clothing is made of plastic, such as this pair of running pants. **Think about which articles of your clothing are made of plastic.**

1   Quick, name ten things that are made of plastic! It shouldn't be too hard. Maybe you named your toothbrush, but you could also include the toothpaste tube. Maybe you thought of seats on a bus, but don't forget the gas tank! And how about the soft bags that hold your groceries or the hard covering on your television? The fact is, plastic is all around us every day.

Fantastic Plastic

2   Once plastic started to be **mass-produced** in the 1950s, it began to replace wood and metal as the primary material for consumer products. That's partly because of the endless variety of shapes plastic can take, but there are other important and practical reasons as well.

3   For one thing, plastic is usually cheaper than the alternatives. Consider the *Paper or plastic?* question often asked at the supermarket. You might be surprised to learn that it takes less energy to produce plastic bags than it does to produce paper bags. Also, plastic bags cost less to transport because each paper bag takes up seven times as much space as a plastic one.

4   Plastic is also very **durable.** Many plastics can absorb the shock of an impact without breaking, which is one reason shampoo bottles are made of plastic and not glass. Plastic can also withstand contact with many harsh chemicals, so it is used to hold household cleaners such as bleach. It's useful for tubes and pipes because it doesn't rust, and because liquid doesn't pass through it, it's also a great material for garbage bags.

5   Let's take a look at what goes into making this extremely **versatile** material.

---

mass-produced (mas'-prə-doōst') made in large quantities by machinery

Connect

Use the information in **paragraph 4** to make a connection. Complete the sentence below.

When I read about how strong plastic is, it

reminds me _____

_____

_____

because _____

_____

_____

What type of connection did you make? You can look back at page 3 for help if you need to.

_____

From the Ground Up

6   The major component of most plastic comes from crude oil, the thick substance found deep in the earth that's also used to produce gasoline. (To read more about gasoline, see *World Works, Level E*, Lesson 3.) After it's pumped from the ground, crude oil goes through a refining process that breaks long chains of **molecules** into smaller chains. Some of these smaller chains are then put through a chemical process that binds them together in new ways to form longer chains called resins.

7   Different combinations of chains of **atoms** result in resins with different properties. It's these different kinds of resins that allow manufacturers to make many different kinds of plastic products. For example, some plastic is colorful and shiny (think plastic plates), while some is transparent (think sandwich bags). And some is rigid (plastic spoons), while some is flexible (drinking straws).

Visualize

Reread **paragraph 7**. Write **two** details from the text that help you visualize different kinds of plastic products.

1. _____

_____

2. _____

_____

Use the details in the text and what you already know to visualize different plastic products and their different properties. Draw what you are visualizing in the box below.

Raw meat in a grocery store is packaged with two kinds of plastic. The plastic foam tray protects the food against freezer burn, and the clear plastic wrapped around the food and the tray protects shoppers from the bacteria on the food. **Think about other uses for plastic foam and clear plastic wrap.**

molecules (mä′-li-kūlz′) the smallest pieces that a substance can be divided into without losing its specific qualities

atoms (a′-təmz) the smallest complete units of any element that can combine with other substances to form **molecules**

8   Raw resins, however, don't necessarily have all the qualities that manufacturers need for their products. To create a product with specific qualities, substances called additives are put in. Different kinds of additives can guarantee long life for plastic products by protecting them from the **adverse** effects of heat, light, and bacteria.

The Heat Is On

9   Heat plays a critical role in making plastic products. The way heat affects the resins depends on which of the two main plastic groups a resin belongs to: thermoplastics or thermosets.

10   The resins in thermoplastics resemble long strings of spaghetti, and they are held together by electrical attraction. Because this attraction is weak, it breaks down easily when heat is applied, causing the resins to become soft. The resins can be molded into a different shape while they are soft, and as they cool they harden into that shape. This heating and cooling process can be done repeatedly, just as a frozen puddle melts and then freezes again. This characteristic makes thermoplastics easy to create and recycle.

11   Unlike thermoplastic resins, thermoset resins harden when they are heated. This is because thermoset resins have specific chains of atoms along their sides that become tangled and bond permanently to each other when heat is applied. Because they harden with heat, thermosets cannot be reheated and reshaped, just as mashed potatoes can't be turned back into regular potatoes. Thermosets are valued because of their strength.

12   To shape plastic products out of thermoplastics and thermosets, manufacturers can use any of several methods.

Get in Shape

13   One common method is called injection molding. During this process, the resin is heated in a chamber until it softens. Then it's injected into a mold, where it cools and becomes solid. This method is used mostly to produce thermoplastics such as yogurt containers or bottle caps.

Ask Questions

Ask yourself a self-check question about **paragraphs 10** and **11**. Look back at the questions listed on page 15 if you need to. Write your question below.

_____

_____

_____

What fix-up strategies could you use to answer your question? Look back at the fix-up strategies listed on page 15 if you need to. Write your answer and your fix-up strategies below.

Answer _____

_____

_____

_____

Fix-Up Strategies _____

_____

_____

_____

83

Reread **paragraph 14**. Write **two** details from the text that help you visualize what the process of extrusion molding looks like.

1. _____

   _____

2. _____

   _____

Use your five senses to visualize these details. Draw what you are visualizing in the box below.

14   If manufacturers need to make thermoplastics such as tubes or food wrap, they use extrusion molding. With this method, soft, heated plastic is squeezed through a small, shaped opening called a die. As it emerges from the die, the plastic is in the shape of the finished product. It's then quickly cooled with cold water or air to keep its new shape.

15   Blow molding is a process that takes extrusion molding a step further. A plastic tube made by using extrusion molding is set inside a mold while it's still soft. Air is blown into the tube, forcing it to take the shape of the surrounding mold. Blow molding is used to make hollow thermoplastics such as milk jugs. Because the end product is a single piece with no seams, it's very strong and not likely to leak or split.

16   To mold thermosets, manufacturers often use compression molding. First the resin is put into a heated mold. Then pressure is applied to squeeze the resin so it fills the mold. Because thermosets harden with heat, the resin solidifies while it's inside the heated mold. Compression molding is used to make products such as light switches and door frames for cars.

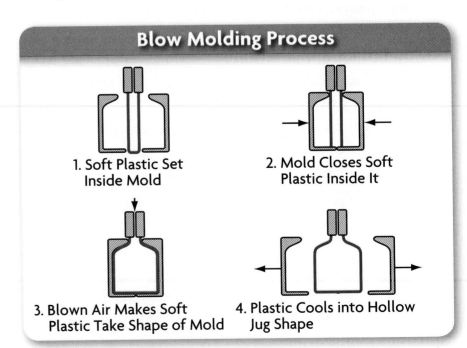

Blowing air into soft plastic inside a mold creates hollow plastic products such as milk jugs. **Think about what other plastic products might be produced by using blow molding.**

Recycle

17   Plastic, while important and useful, does have a **downside.** It can take an extremely long time for plastic to decompose, or break down into elements that can be absorbed into nature. Just think of those plastic grocery bags you use—it will take about one thousand years before they even start to decompose. As time goes on, discarded plastic takes up more and more space, which is alarming when you think about how many plastic products are out there.

18   Scientists and manufacturers are trying to find ways to fix the environmental problems with plastic. They're developing plastics that are photodegradable, which means they decompose in sunlight, as well as biodegradable, which means they'll break down much more quickly than they normally do. They're also making sure more plastics are recyclable.

19   And this is where you can help: next time you toss out a water bottle or any other of the many plastic items that are used every day, aim for the recycling bin instead of the trash can. You'll be doing your part to take care of the environment.

Did You Know?

Plastic makes life easier, but can it also make life safer? Consider these facts:

- Plastic bicycle helmets reduce the risk of head injury by 85 percent.
- More than 1,900 police officers' lives have been saved by bullet-resistant plastic vests.
- **Disposable** plastic tubes and bags help hospitals maintain a **sterile** environment.

---

sterile (ster'-əl) clean and free from bacteria

My WORKSPACE

The arrows forming a triangle let you know the product is recyclable. The number and the letters refer to the type of plastic the product is made of. **Think about places you've been that provide special containers for products that can be recycled.**

Self-Check
Look back at the question you wrote on page 80.
- Does the information in the text answer your question? If it does, what is the answer? If it does not, where could you look to find more information?

Write your answers on a separate sheet of paper.

85

Understanding What You Read

Fill in the circle next to the correct answer. You may look back at the text to help you choose the correct answers.

1. Which sentence **best** states the main idea of the "Fantastic Plastic" section?
   ○ A. Plastic is a popular material with many positive qualities.
   ○ B. Many plastics can absorb shock without breaking.
   ○ C. Plastic is cheaper to produce than paper.

2. The major component of most plastic comes from
   ○ A. crude oil.
   ○ B. electricity.
   ○ C. light and bacteria.

3. Extrusion molding and compression molding are different because only extrusion molding
   ○ A. uses heat to make plastic products.
   ○ B. is used to make soft plastic products.
   ○ C. can produce plastic products with different shapes.

4. The diagram titled "Blow Molding Process" helps support the author's point that
   ○ A. a plastic product with no seams is not likely to leak or split.
   ○ B. heat affects thermosets and thermoplastics differently.
   ○ C. air is blown into the soft plastic tube inside the mold.

5. From the information in the "Recycle" section, you can infer that
   ○ A. most scientists and manufacturers don't like to recycle.
   ○ B. plastic products cause problems with the environment.
   ○ C. sunlight can damage most of the plastics we use today.

Score 4 points for each correct answer.

_____/20 **Total Score: Activity A**

Asking Questions and Visualizing

Paragraph 17 from the article is shown below. Read the paragraph. Then use the paragraph to complete the activities.

>   Plastic, while important and useful, does have a downside. It can take an extremely long time for plastic to decompose, or break down into elements that can be absorbed into nature. Just think of those plastic grocery bags you use—it will take about one thousand years before they even start to decompose. As time goes on, discarded plastic takes up more and more space, which is alarming when you think about how many plastic products are out there.

1. Think of a good question to ask yourself to check your understanding of the paragraph. Write your self-check question below. Then write the answer to your question and the fix-up strategies you used.

Self-Check Question _____

_____

Answer _____

_____

Fix-Up Strategies _____

_____

2. Study the details in the paragraph above. Then use the details, what you already know, and your imagination to create a picture in your mind. Draw what you are visualizing in the box below.

```

```

Score 5 points each for numbers 1 and 2.

_____ /10   **Total Score: Activity B**

Using Words

Complete the analogies below by writing a word from the box on each line. Remember that in an analogy, the last two words or phrases must be related in the same way that the first two are related.

> **durable**   **versatile**   **adverse**
>
> **downside**   **disposable**

1. fancy dishes : paper plates : : collectible : _____

2. cheerful : good news : : discouraged : _____

3. good flavors : delicious : : many uses : _____

4. wet : dry : : fragile : _____

5. near : close : : damaging : _____

Choose one word from the box. Write a sentence using the word. Be sure to put at least one detail in your sentence. The detail should show that you understand what the word means.

6. _____

_____

Writing About It

Make a Connection Think about what you know about plastic from your own experiences. Think about the plastic items in your home and school that you use every day. Then make a connection to the text. Finish the sentences below to describe your connection. Be sure your writing matches the information in the text. Use the checklist on page 119 to check your work.

When I read about _____

_____

in the article, it reminded me _____

_____

_____

because _____

_____

_____

Making this connection helped me understand _____

_____

_____

_____

WE RECYCLE

Lesson 7 Add your scores from activities A, B, and C to get your total score.

_____ **A** Understanding What You Read

_____ **B** Asking Questions and Visualizing

_____ **C** Using Words

_____ **Total Score**

Multiply your **Total Score x 2** _____

This is your percentage score.

Record your percentage score on the graph on page 121.

Hybrid Cars
The Drive Toward a Solution

Hybrid cars can do just about everything regular cars can do—and they burn less gas.

READING SKILL **Reviewing the Reading Skills**

You practiced three reading skills in Unit Two. Rate your understanding of each skill using the chart below. Use the following rating scale:

3   I understand this skill well. I use it easily and correctly while I read.

2   I understand this skill a little bit. I sometimes use it correctly while I read.

1   I don't understand this skill. I am not able to use it while I read.

Mark the box under the number 3, 2, or 1 for each skill.

	3	**2**	**1**	**Need to review?**		**Turn to:**
Finding the Main Idea and Details				Yes	No	Lesson 4, page 41
Taking Notes				Yes	No	Lesson 5, page 53
Summarizing				Yes	No	Lesson 6, page 65

If you rated your understanding of a skill at 2 or 1, look back at the lesson page where that skill was taught. The lesson page is shown in the chart above. Reread the skill definition and the example. This will help you get ready to complete the next lesson.

After you have reviewed the skills, complete the sentences below.

The skill I find most helpful when reading is _____

because _____

_____

During this lesson, one thing I can do to improve my reading is _____

_____

_____

Getting Ready to Read

Think About What You Know

CONNECT Think about cars and gasoline. What are the advantages of using gas-powered cars? What are the disadvantages? Write your answers here.

_____

_____

_____

Word Power

PREVIEW Read the words and definitions below. Then look ahead at the title and at the headings and images in the article.

consumption (kən-səmp'-shən)	the amount of something, such as gasoline or electricity, that is used
emit (ē-mit')	to give off or send out
fundamental (fən'-də-men'-təl)	having to do with the most basic or most important parts of something
disperse (di-spərs')	to break up something and send the pieces in different directions
innovations (i'-nə-vā'-shənz)	ideas, methods, or devices that are new

PREDICT Use the words, title, headings, and images to make a prediction. What do you think the author will say about hybrid cars?

I predict the author will _____

_____

because _____

_____

Reason to Read

Read to find out if the prediction you wrote above matches the information in the text. At the end of the article, you will be asked about your prediction. You will need to explain how your prediction is the same as the text or different from it.

Hybrid Cars
The Drive Toward a Solution

1   Did you know that in the United States we burn more than 400 million gallons of gasoline every day, mostly to power our vehicles? In fact, per person we use more than five times as much gas as people who live in Europe.

2   When gas is less expensive, we tend not to worry about how much of it we burn. However, when prices increase—or when we come to terms with the fact that burning gasoline has a negative effect on the environment—we begin searching for ways to reduce our gasoline **consumption.** One option some people have embraced is the hybrid car.

What's a Hybrid?

3   A hybrid is a combination of two or more different things; today's hybrid cars combine a gasoline engine and an electric motor. This design allows a hybrid to use less gasoline and **emit** less pollution into the air. To understand exactly how a hybrid car works, let's take a look at two kinds of cars.

Gasoline: Power at a Price

4   The engine in a traditional gas-powered car is called an internal combustion engine (ICE). That's because the combustion, or burning, of gas takes place inside the engine. In there gasoline mixes with air and is ignited by a spark from a spark plug. This causes a series of tiny explosions that push **pistons** up and down inside thick metal tubes called cylinders. The pistons' movement creates the power to turn the wheels, which moves the vehicle.

---

pistons (pis′-tənz) metal discs that are part of an engine and that move up and down to power the movement of other parts

Take Notes
Get ready to take two-column notes.

- Get two blank sheets of paper.
- Draw a line from the top to the bottom of each page. Make the left column narrower than the right column.
- As you read, write the main ideas and topics in the left column. Write details and definitions in the right column.
- Make sure to take notes on **at least two** main ideas or topics for each page of text.

Gas-powered vehicles play a very large role in our society. **Think about the many different ways gas-powered vehicles are used by individuals and businesses.**

Looking under the hood of this hybrid car, you can see the top of the ICE on the left. In this model, the electric motor is below the ICE. **Think about how taking care of a hybrid car might be different than taking care of a traditional car.**

Take Notes and Summarize

Reread **paragraph 5**. In the left column of your two-column notes, write the topics "benefits of gas-powered cars" and "drawbacks of gas-powered cars." In the right column, write details from the text that support each topic.

Then use your notes to help you write a summary of paragraph 5 below.

_____

_____

_____

_____

_____

_____

94

5 There are many wonderful things about gas-powered cars: they can go hundreds of miles before having to be refueled, they can **accelerate** quickly, and they can attain high cruising speeds. Some cars, however, get only about 15 to 20 miles per gallon of gasoline. In addition, burning gasoline produces gases—particularly carbon dioxide—that pollute the air. Burning just one gallon of gasoline produces nearly 20 pounds of carbon dioxide. This is significant because most scientists today cite rising levels of certain gases in the atmosphere as a contributing factor in **global warming.**

Electric Cars? Not So Fast.

6 You might be surprised to know that the first electric cars were produced more than a hundred years ago. Today some car manufacturers still continue to develop and market electric cars.

7 Electric cars emit hardly any pollutants, but the reason you don't see more people driving them is that they too have some **fundamental** problems. An electric car has an electric motor that is powered by a group of large batteries. As with all batteries, electric car batteries lose energy with use. So an electric car owner must periodically plug the car into an electric outlet to recharge the batteries. The trouble with this is that the process of recharging can take eight or nine hours and must be completed every 50 to 100 miles. Unfortunately, this does not suit many people's travel needs or lifestyle.

8 Another issue is speed. Many electric cars can reach a maximum speed of only 35 or 40 miles per hour, which is not fast enough to keep pace with traffic on an expressway.

9 Keeping all these things in mind, some car manufacturers figured out a way to use the strengths of each type of car to overcome the weaknesses of the other—and they created the hybrid solution.

accelerate (ik-seʹ-lə-rātʹ) to gain speed
global warming (glōʹ-bəl-wôrʹ-ming) an increase in the average temperatures of the earth that is caused by certain gases released into the air

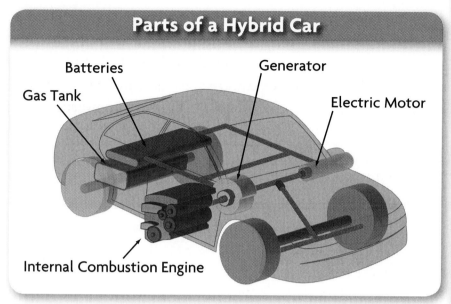

Parts of a Hybrid Car

Batteries

Generator

Gas Tank

Electric Motor

Internal Combustion Engine

This diagram shows the basic parts of one type of hybrid car. Notice the generator, electic motor, and batteries. **Think about why the electric motor and the generator need to be connected to the batteries.**

Best of Both Worlds

10   Today's hybrids go fast enough to keep up with traffic on the highway, yet they offer as much as twice the fuel-efficiency of many traditional cars. How can hybrids use less fuel? The secret lies primarily in the size of the gas-powered ICE. The ICE in a hybrid car is more fuel-efficient than the ICE in a traditional car. Why? Because it's much smaller.

11   Larger ICEs have more cylinders and heavier pistons to fire. This also means the car itself is much heavier. These factors all make a car burn more fuel.

12   ICEs in traditional cars are often built large enough to accelerate the car quickly and reach speeds that a driver would really only need if he or she decided to drive the car on a racetrack! On the other hand, the ICEs in hybrid cars are much more practical; they're sized to match the driver's average need for power instead of the maximum need.

Find the Main Idea and Take Notes

Review **paragraphs 10, 11, and 12.** Write the topic or main idea of these three paragraphs.

_____

_____

_____

In the left column of your notes, write the topic or main idea as a short, precise phrase. In the right column, write three details from the paragraphs that support the topic or main idea.

Take Notes and Summarize

Reread **paragraph 13**. In the left column of your notes, write the topic or main idea of the paragraph. Write supporting details in the right column. Remember to use short, precise phrases in your notes.

Then use your notes to write a summary of paragraph 13 below. Remember that your summmary should be about 20 words or less.

_____

_____

_____

_____

_____

_____

13 So how can a hybrid car have a smaller ICE and still keep up with traditional cars on the expressway? The answer has to do with the electric motor. When the hybrid needs an extra boost to accelerate quickly or climb a steep hill, the electric motor automatically kicks in to share the burden of powering the car. When the car reaches a level cruising speed, the electric motor turns off.

14 Hybrid cars have a few other gas-saving secrets too. One of them is that the ICE automatically shuts down whenever the vehicle comes to a complete stop and restarts as soon as the driver presses the accelerator. As a result, no gasoline is wasted while the car idles at a traffic light or sits in a traffic jam.

Take the Long Road

15 Another intriguing feature of the hybrid car is its ability to capture and store its own energy. Hybrid car manufacturers figured out that by incorporating a **generator** that is connected to the wheel axles, they could create a system called regenerative braking.

Comparing Cars			
Type of Car	Miles Per Gallon (city)	Miles Per Gallon (highway)	Greenhouse Gases Released (in tons per year)
large gas SUV	13	20	11.7
large gas van	19	26	8.6
mid-size gas sedan	20	27	8.1
small gas sedan	30	40	5.5
small hybrid sedan	60	51	3.4

Greenhouse gases are the gases in the air that cause global warming. **Think about how these five types of cars compare in terms of greenhouse gases and global warming.**

generator (je'-nə-rā'-tər) a machine that makes electricity

16   When you step on the brakes in a traditional vehicle, the brakes transfer the energy of forward motion into friction heat and **disperse** it into the air—so all that energy is lost. The braking system in a hybrid, however, is designed to channel this energy into the generator (in some hybrids, the electric motor acts as the generator), which then transfers the energy into the batteries to be stored. And the batteries recharge while the car is in motion, so there's never a need to stop and plug in the car.

17   Thanks to these **innovations,** some hybrids can get up to 60 miles per gallon—more than twice as much as most traditional cars. So what's it like to drive a hybrid car?

Quiet Riding

18   On the road, hybrids handle like ordinary cars. The interplay between the ICE and electric motor is so seamless you don't even notice it. However, you will notice the difference in sound. Hybrid cars tend to run much more quietly than traditional cars. In fact, sometimes you won't even hear them coming. So make sure you always look both ways before crossing the street!

19   Car manufacturers continue to experiment with fuel alternatives such as hydrogen, **ethanol,** and natural gas to power vehicles. So hybrid cars probably won't be our last stop on the road to energy-efficient transportation. However, they do offer a current option for drivers who are concerned about the environment and who want to burn less gas.

ethanol (e′-thə-nôl′) a type of fuel made from grains and other plants that can be mixed with gasoline to power cars

Many hybrid cars are shaped to reduce wind resistance, and many have tires that inflate to a high pressure to reduce friction resistance against the road. **Think about why makers of hybrid cars would add these special features.**

Take Notes

When you are finished reading the article, review your notes. You can use your notes to help you complete the activities on pages 98–101.

Self-Check

Look back at the prediction you wrote on page 92.
- Does your prediction match the text? Why or why not?

Write your answers on a separate sheet of paper.

Understanding What You Read

Fill in the circle next to the correct answer. You may look back at the text to help you choose the correct answers.

1. Which step has to happen **before** the pistons in an ICE start moving?
- ○ A. The wheels begin to turn.
- ○ B. The spark plugs make sparks.
- ○ C. The car reaches maximum speed.

2. What problem with smaller ICEs does the electric motor solve?
- ○ A. Cars with smaller ICEs cannot accelerate as quickly.
- ○ B. Cars with smaller ICEs must be recharged often.
- ○ C. Cars with smaller ICEs are not very heavy.

3. When the hybrid needs an extra boost to accelerate quickly or climb a steep hill, the
- ○ A. ICE begins to work harder and burn more gas.
- ○ B. brakes transfer power to the generator.
- ○ C. electric motor automatically kicks in.

4. From the chart titled "Comparing Cars," you can conclude that
- ○ A. gas burned in hybrid cars does not contribute to global warming.
- ○ B. most gas-powered cars release fewer greenhouse gases than hybrid cars do.
- ○ C. driving a large SUV contributes more to global warming than driving a sedan does.

5. From the "Quiet Riding" section, you can infer that
- ○ A. hybrid cars could pose an added danger to people such as cyclists or pedestrians who are blind.
- ○ B. hybrid cars will always be the best option for drivers who are concerned about global warming.
- ○ C. after buying a hybrid car, it would take awhile for even an experienced driver to learn how to drive it.

Score 4 points for each correct answer.

_____/20 **Total Score: Activity A**

Finding the Main Idea and Details and Taking Notes

Paragraph 14 from the article is shown below. Read the paragraph. Then use the paragraph to complete the activities.

> Hybrid cars have a few other gas-saving secrets too. One of them is that the ICE automatically shuts down whenever the vehicle comes to a complete stop and restarts as soon as the driver presses the accelerator. As a result, no gasoline is wasted while the car idles at a traffic light or sits in a traffic jam.

1. Fill in the circle next to the phrase that **best** states the topic of the paragraph.
- ○ A. how the ICE shuts down
- ○ B. the reason no gasoline is wasted
- ○ C. another way hybrid cars save gas

2. Use the notebook page below to show how you would take two-column notes on the paragraph. Write the topic of the paragraph and **three** details that support it.

Score 5 points each for numbers 1 and 2.

_____ /10   **Total Score: Activity B**

Using Words

Complete each sentence with a word from the box. Write the missing word on the line.

consumption	emit	fundamental
disperse	innovations	

1. In science class, we learned about _____ in medicine that might help people stay healthy longer.

2. Reading and writing are _____ skills that are the building blocks of education.

3. After the sun and wind _____ the fog, it will be easier for the driver to see the road.

4. Instead of selling our crops, we keep the food for our own

   _____.

5. These small lamps don't _____ very much light.

Choose one word from the box. Write a new sentence using the word. Be sure to put at least one detail in your sentence. The detail should show that you understand what the word means. Use the sentences above as examples.

6. _____

   _____

Score 4 points for each correct answer in numbers 1–5.

(Do not score number 6.)

_____ /20 **Total Score: Activity C**

Writing About It

Write a Summary Use your two-column notes to write a summary of the article you just read about hybrid cars. Finish the sentences below to write your summary. Your summary should include the most important ideas from the text. Use the checklist on page 119 to check your work.

Hybrid cars combine the benefits of _____

_____

Carmakers developed hybrid cars because _____

_____

_____

Electric cars _____

_____

_____

The main reason hybrid cars can use less gas is _____

_____

_____

_____

Other gas-saving features of hybrid cars include _____

_____

_____

_____

Lesson 8 Add your scores from activities A, B, and C to get your total score.

_____ **A** Understanding What You Read

_____ **B** Finding the Main Idea and Details and Taking Notes

_____ **C** Using Words

_____ **Total Score**   Multiply your **Total Score x 2** _____

This is your percentage score.

Record your percentage score on the graph on page 121.

LANDFILLS
Let's Talk Trash

Most of the garbage created in the United States is put into landfills.

READING SKILL **Reviewing the Reading Skills**

You practiced six reading skills in this book. Rate your understanding of each skill using the chart below. Use the following rating scale:

3 I understand this skill well. I use it easily and correctly while I read.

2 I understand this skill a little bit. I sometimes use it correctly while I read.

1 I don't understand this skill. I am not able to use it while I read.

Mark the box under the number 3, 2, or 1 for each skill.

	3	2	1	Need to review?		Turn to:
Making Connections				Yes	No	Lesson 1, page 3
Asking Questions				Yes	No	Lesson 2, page 15
Visualizing				Yes	No	Lesson 3, page 27
Finding the Main Idea and Details				Yes	No	Lesson 4, page 41
Taking Notes				Yes	No	Lesson 5, page 53
Summarizing				Yes	No	Lesson 6, page 65

If you rated your understanding of a skill at 2 or 1, look back at the lesson page where that skill was taught. The lesson page is shown in the chart above. Reread the skill definition and the example. This will help you get ready to complete the next lesson. After you have reviewed the skills, complete the sentences below.

The skill I find most helpful when reading is _____

because _____

_____

During this lesson, one thing I can do to improve my reading is _____

_____

_____

Getting Ready to Read

Think About What You Know

CONNECT Think about the last time you threw something away. What was it? What do you think happens to trash after the garbage collectors haul it away? Write your answers here.

_____

_____

_____

Word Power

PREVIEW Read the words and definitions below. Then look ahead at the title and at the headings and images in the article.

conserve (kən-sərv′)	to use as little of something as possible to avoid wasting it
decompose (dē′-kəm-pōz′)	to decay or rot
legible (le′-jə-bəl)	clear enough for someone to read
sanitized (sa′-nə-tīzd′)	cleaned very well to get rid of dirt and germs
embedded (im-be′-dəd)	set firmly and deeply into the surrounding substance

QUESTION Use the words, title, headings, and images to ask a question. What would you like to know about landfills? Write your question on the lines below.

_____

_____

_____

Reason to Read

Read to find out if the information in the text answers your question. At the end of the article, you will be asked to look back at your question. You will decide whether or not your question is answered in the text.

LANDFILLS
Let's Talk Trash

1   Think about all the empty soda cans, leftover food, old magazines, used paper, and broken or worn-out objects you discard. You bundle them up neatly and leave them for the garbage collectors to carry away. But where does your garbage go? Most of it goes into a landfill.

Not a Dump

2   A landfill is a structure that's specially designed to contain and isolate trash so that the trash doesn't threaten public health. A landfill's primary purpose is to prevent trash from polluting groundwater, which is the water in underground lakes, streams, and springs—the water that most communities depend on for their drinking water.

3   Modern landfills have been around for only about 30 years. Before the existence of landfills, a community took care of its trash by dumping it into a giant hole in the ground and leaving it exposed. These uncovered heaps of rotting garbage fostered the spread of germs and attracted disease-carrying rodents. They also allowed poisonous materials from the trash to seep into the earth and eventually into the groundwater.

4   People began to realize that dumps were a threat to public health. So in 1976, Congress passed the Resource Conservation and Recovery Act. This law called for an end to traditional dumps and for the proper management of Municipal Solid Waste (MSW) landfills. Today there are about 1,500 MSW landfills in the United States. Let's find out how they work.

Take Notes

Get ready to take two-column notes.

- Get two blank sheets of paper.
- Draw a line from the top to the bottom of each page. Make the left column narrower than the right column.
- As you read, write the main ideas and topics in the left column. Write details and definitions in the right column.
- Make sure to take notes on **at least two** main ideas or topics for each page of text.

Reread **paragraph 5**. What is the main idea of this paragraph?

_____

_____

In the left column of your notes, write the main idea as a short phrase. In the right column, write three details from the paragraph that support the main idea.

Trash Goes In

5   An MSW landfill is like a giant bathtub built into or above the ground and divided into many individual sections called **refuse** cells. For better control of the space, one cell is filled at a time. As trash is deposited into a cell, workers spread it out and compact it into a thin layer using tractors and other heavy equipment. Typically, the trash is compressed to about 25 percent of its original volume to **conserve** space.

6   Each evening trash is covered with six inches (15 cm) of soil. This eliminates windblown litter and foul odors and keeps out birds, rats, and other animals overnight. To save space, workers remove the soil the next day before depositing more trash.

7   Once all the refuse cells are filled, a plastic or clay barrier is placed over all the cells to reduce the amount of water that gets into them. A permanent layer of soil—several feet thick—is added, and grass or vines are planted in it to prevent erosion, or destruction, of the soil. Then the landfill is closed.

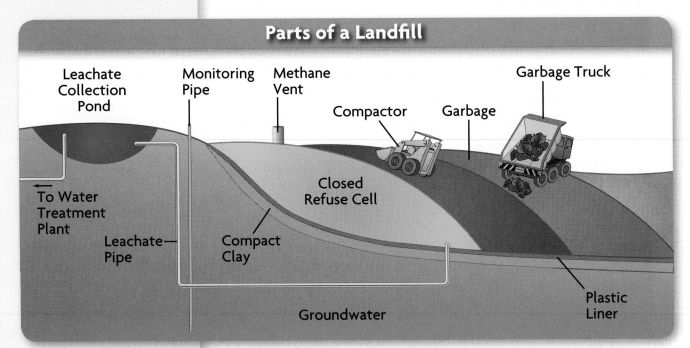

Parts of a Landfill

Leachate Collection Pond — Monitoring Pipe — Methane Vent — Compactor — Garbage — Garbage Truck

To Water Treatment Plant — Leachate Pipe — Compact Clay — Closed Refuse Cell — Groundwater — Plastic Liner

This diagram shows a cross section of a landfill and its parts. **Think about the purpose of each part of the landfill.**

refuse (reʹ-fūsʹ) something that has been thrown away; garbage

8   In addition to the actual area where the trash is deposited, each landfill also has a strip of land around its **perimeter** that separates the trash from the surrounding area and provides space for landfill maintenance activities.

9   Because of the way trash is compressed and covered in a landfill, it does not **decompose** the way it normally would if it were spread out and exposed to oxygen and water. In fact, the landfill's design actually preserves the trash. For example, decades after being deposited in landfills, newspapers have been pulled out with the paper intact and the print still **legible.**

The Issue of Water

10   Because of the environmental hazards associated with trash, landfills must be carefully constructed and maintained. Rainwater poses a special maintenance problem: any water that gets into the landfill will filter down through the trash, picking up **contaminants** along the way. The resulting contaminated water is called leachate. The more water that gets into the landfill, the greater the chances are that leachate will leak out, mix with groundwater, and pose a threat to humans, plants, and animals.

11   To keep water out, MSW landfills have drainage systems that channel rainwater away from the landfill before it reaches the trash. However, no drainage system can keep out all water—leachate will always be present. To contain the leachate, MSW landfills have a bottom lining. The lining might consist of a layer several feet deep of highly compressed clay, a very strong plastic sheet, or a combination of the two. Then pipes are placed inside the landfill to drain the leachate.

12   Leachate may travel directly through sewers to the local water treatment plant to be **sanitized.** If the leachate is especially toxic, it flows into collection ponds first to be filtered and/or pretreated before it's released to the treatment plant.

---

perimeter (pə-ri′-mə-tər) the border or boundary of a specific area
contaminants (kən-ta′-mə-nənts) substances that make something unclean or unfit for use

In some communities, trash goes first to a transfer or relay station to be sorted and sometimes compacted. Later it's trucked to the landfill. **Think about the amount of gasoline that is burned while trucking garbage to landfills.**

Visualize

Reread **paragraph 10.** Write **two** details from the text that help you visualize how rainwater becomes leachate.

1. _____

   _____

2. _____

   _____

Use the details in the text to visualize. Draw what you are visualizing in the box below.

Flares like this one burn off methane gas as it's released from the landfill. **Think about the benefits of using methane for fuel instead of burning it**.

Connect

Use the information in **paragraph 18** to make a connection. Complete the sentence below.

When I read about _____

_____

_____

it reminds me _____

_____

_____

because _____

_____

_____

13   How do landfill managers know if the liners and drainage systems are working? The groundwater around a landfill is monitored regularly for the presence of certain chemicals, temperature changes, and other problem signs. If certain chemicals are present in the groundwater, it means that the landfill is probably leaking and that landfill managers need to locate and stop the leak.

14   Some scientists are concerned that even the strongest liners will eventually wear out and begin to leak. This is why there are laws that require landfill managers to monitor landfills for a minimum of 30 years after they are filled and closed.

Dangerous Gases

15   Another maintenance issue with landfills is methane gas. This gas is created by bacteria that feed on the rotting garbage. Methane poses a danger because it can get trapped inside the landfill and catch fire—or even explode. To reduce the risk of fires and explosions, landfill operators vent the gas through vertical pipes **embedded** in the landfill.

16   Methane is a powerful **greenhouse gas**; to reduce its impact on the environment, it's usually burned off as it is released. At some landfills, however, the gas is collected to fuel generators, which create electricity, or boilers, which create heat.

17   As more and more people become aware of where trash goes and what becomes of it, there is a greater demand for better solutions. One solution is recycling.

Get Smart About Trash

18   Around the time people started building landfills instead of more dumps, many communities also created recycling programs. Recycling things such as plastic, paper, aluminum, and glass conserves natural resources and reduces trash. (You read about recycling plastics in Lesson 7 of this book.)

greenhouse gas (grēn'-hows-gas') a gas that traps heat from the sun in Earth's atmosphere and contributes to global warming

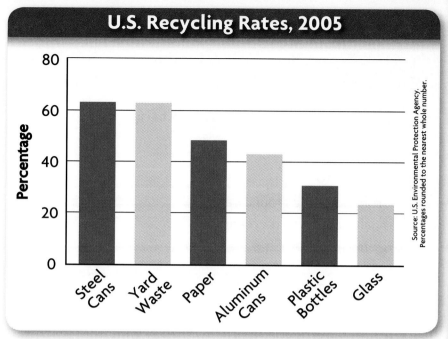

U.S. Recycling Rates, 2005

Source: U.S. Environmental Protection Agency. Percentages rounded to the nearest whole number.

This bar graph shows the recycling rates for six different items. For recycling rates to increase, more people and businesses need to use products made from recycled materials. **Think about products sold in stores that are made from recycled paper, such as toilet tissue or paper napkins.**

19   **Composting** material that comes from living things such as food scraps and plant matter is another good way to reduce trash in landfills. This type of waste tends to decompose very quickly when it's not put into a landfill. Many towns require yard waste such as tree trimmings and grass clippings to be collected separately so they can be composted and used as fertilizer.

20   You can do your part to reduce trash by cutting down on the amount of packaged products you use; reusing plastic bags, plastic bottles, and glass jars; recycling as much as possible; and purchasing products made from recycled materials. Landfills are only one part of the solution to protecting our environment—the rest is up to us.

By the Numbers
The United States generates about *twice as much* garbage per person as most of the other developed countries in the world.

composting (käm'-pōst'-ing) gathering plant matter and some types of food refuse and allowing the materials to break down naturally so that they can be mixed back into the soil

Take Notes and Summarize
Reread **paragraph 19.** In the left column of your notes, write the main idea or topic of the paragraph. Write the details in the right column. Remember to use short, precise phrases.

Then use your notes to write a summary of paragraph 19 below.

_____
_____
_____
_____
_____
_____

Self-Check
Look back at the question you wrote on page 104.
• Does the information in the text answer your question? If it does, what is the answer? If it does not, where could you look to find more information?
Write your answers on a separate sheet of paper.

Understanding What You Read

Fill in the circle next to the correct answer. You may look back at the text to help you choose the correct answers.

1. A landfill's primary purpose is to
   - ○ A. prevent trash from polluting groundwater.
   - ○ B. provide an easy alternative to recycling.
   - ○ C. generate energy from methane gas.

2. Which step is completed each day **before** trash is covered with soil?
   - ○ A. Windblown litter is collected.
   - ○ B. The trash in the cell is compacted.
   - ○ C. A plastic barrier is placed over the trash.

3. The diagram titled "Parts of a Landfill" helps support the author's point that
   - ○ A. some landfills collect methane gas for fuel.
   - ○ B. landfills are specially designed to contain and isolate trash.
   - ○ C. modern landfills have been around for only about 30 years.

4. From the photo caption on page 107, you can infer that
   - ○ A. the more garbage we move, the more we pollute the air.
   - ○ B. most landfills are built near the neighborhoods that use them.
   - ○ C. if we create more garbage transfer stations, we can solve more garbage problems.

5. What is one effect of rainwater getting into landfills?
   - ○ A. Chemicals must be put into the landfill.
   - ○ B. Methane gas escapes from the landfill.
   - ○ C. Leachate forms in the landfill.

Score 4 points for each correct answer.

_____/20   **Total Score: Activity A**

Finding the Main Idea and Details and Summarizing

Paragraph 4 from the article is shown below. Read the paragraph. Then use the paragraph to complete the activities.

> People began to realize that dumps were a threat to public health. So in 1976, Congress passed the Resource Conservation and Recovery Act. This law called for an end to traditional dumps and for the proper management of Municipal Solid Waste (MSW) landfills. Today there are about 1,500 MSW landfills in the United States. Let's find out how they work.

1. Fill in the circle next to the sentence that **best** states the main idea of the paragraph.

   ○ A. Landfills replaced traditional dumps.
   ○ B. There are about 1,500 MSW landfills.
   ○ C. Congress passed the Resource Conservation and Recovery Act.

2. Complete a summary diagram for the paragraph above. Write the most important ideas from the paragraph in the top boxes. Then write your summary in the bottom box. Remember that your summary should be about 20 words or less.

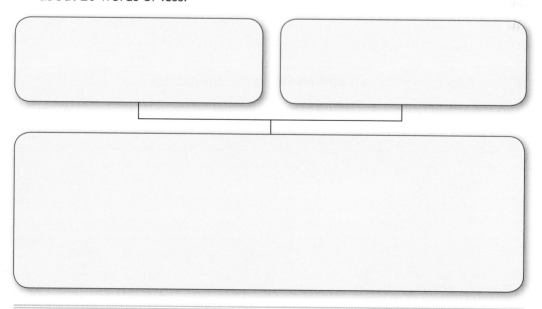

Score 5 points each for numbers 1 and 2.

_____ /10   **Total Score: Activity B**

Using Words

Follow the instructions below. Write your answers on the lines.

1. List **two** things you could do to **conserve** water.

_____

_____

2. List **three** things that could happen as an apple begins to **decompose.**

_____

_____

_____

3. List **two** reasons why your writing needs to be **legible.**

_____

_____

4. List **two** things that are usually **sanitized.**

_____

_____

5. List **two** things that are **embedded** in the ground near your school.

_____

_____

Score 4 points for each correct answer.

_____ /20   **Total Score: Activity C**

Writing About It

Describe What You Are Visualizing Think about the way that landfills were explained in the text. Use your five senses to visualize a landfill. Finish the sentences below to write a description of what you are visualizing. Be sure your writing matches the information in the text. Use the checklist on page 119 to check your work.

The landfill looks _____

_____

_____

The landfill smells _____

_____

_____

The landfill sounds _____

_____

_____

Another thing I can visualize about the landfill is _____

_____

_____

_____

_____

_____

Lesson 9 Add your scores from activities A, B, and C to get your total score.

_____ **A** Understanding What You Read
_____ **B** Finding the Main Idea and Details and Summarizing
_____ **C** Using Words
_____ **Total Score**   Multiply your **Total Score x 2** _____
                                     This is your percentage score.
                     Record your percentage score on the graph on page 121.

Compare and Contrast

You read three articles about everyday things in Unit Three. Think about the topic of each article. Then choose **two** of the articles. Write the titles of the articles in the first two boxes below. Draw pictures in the first two boxes that show how the topics are different in the way they affect people's lives. In the bottom box, draw a picture that shows how the topics are similar in the way they affect people's lives. Label the important parts of your drawings.

Title _____

Title _____

Both

Use your drawings to write a summary of how these everyday things are alike and different. Finish the sentences below to write your summary.

_____ and _____ are different

because _____

_____

_____ and _____ are similar

because _____

_____

Glossary

A

activate (ak′-tə-vāt′) to cause a process to begin working *p. 67*

adverse (ad′-vərs′) harmful or not helpful *p. 83*

B

benefit (be′-nə-fit′) to receive an advantage *p. 9*

C

chronic (krä′-nik) lasting for a long time or happening frequently *p. 45*

conserve (kən-sərv′) to use as little of something as possible to avoid wasting it *p. 106*

consumption (kən-səmp′-shən) the amount of something, such as gasoline or electricity, that is used *p. 93*

correlation (kôr′-ə-lā′-shən) a connection between ideas or events that suggests one might be the cause of the other *p. 46*

D

debilitating (di-bi′-lə-tāt′-ing) causing illness or the loss of strength *p. 45*

decompose (dē′-kəm-pōz′) to decay or rot *p. 107*

deleted (di-lēt′-əd) erased *p. 21*

disperse (di-spərs′) to break up something and send the pieces in different directions *p. 97*

disposable (di-spō′-zə-bəl) made to be thrown away after being used once or only a few times *p. 85*

downside (down′-sīd′) a negative aspect of something *p. 85*

durable (door′-ə-bəl) able to stay in good shape even if used a lot *p. 81*

E

eliminate (i-li′-mə-nāt′) to remove something because it's not necessary *p. 7*

Law Enforcement

embedded (im-be'-dəd) set firmly and deeply into the surrounding substance *p. 108*

emit (ē-mit') to give off or send out *p. 93*

eradicate (i-ra'-də-kāt') to completely stop or eliminate something *p. 59*

evaluation (i-val'-yə-wā'-shən) the process of determining the importance of something *p. 9*

extracted (ik-strakt'-əd) carefully removed using a machine or a chemical process *p. 43*

F

feedback (fēd'-bak') comments made in response to something that's been done *p. 30*

fundamental (fən'-də-men'-təl) having to do with the most basic or most important parts of something *p. 94*

H

highlight (hī'-līt') to direct special attention to something *p. 20*

I

immunity (i-mū'-nə-tē) the ability of a living thing to resist disease *p. 57*

incorporated (in-kôr'-pə-rāt'-əd) joined with something else to form a new whole *p. 32*

ingested (in-jest'-əd) taken into the body by eating or drinking *p. 43*

innovations (i'-nə-vā'-shənz) ideas, methods, or devices that are new *p. 97*

insignificant (in'-sig-ni'-fi-kənt) not important *p. 6*

invaluable (in-val'-yə-bəl) having great value or use *p. 33*

L

legible (le'-jə-bəl) clear enough for someone to read *p. 107*

lethal (lē'-thəl) able to cause death *p. 67*

M

minimize (mi'-nə-mīz') to reduce to the smallest possible amount *p. 7*

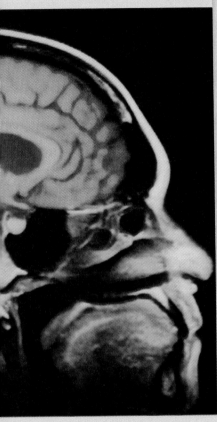

Health

mutate (mū'-tāt') to change in form or structure *p. 59*

O

obscure (əb-skyoor') not well known *p. 67*

omitted (ō-mit'-əd) left something out, either on purpose or by accident *p. 30*

outbreaks (owt'-brāks') sudden increases in the number of people experiencing a disease *p. 58*

P

proficiency (prə-fi'-shən-sē) the ability to do something well *p. 18*

R

receding (ri-sēd'-ing) moving back from an original location *p. 33*

resistant (ri-zis'-tənt) able to remain unharmed or unaffected by something *p. 67*

revert (ri-vərt') to go back to a previous form or way of being *p. 67*

S

sanitized (sa'-nə-tīzd') cleaned very well to get rid of dirt and germs *p. 107*

T

tainted (tānt'-əd) touched or affected by something harmful *p. 56*

U

update (əp'-dāt') to make sure the information for something is current and accurate *p. 19*

V

versatile (vər'-sə-təl) having a large variety of uses *p. 81*

W

widespread (wīd'-spred') happening in many places and among many people *p. 17*

Everyday Things

Pronunciation Guide

a	mat	oo	look
ä	father	ōō	food
ā	date	oi	noise
ch	chin	ow	out
e	wet	ə	pencil
ē	see	sh	sugar
i	tip	th	think
ī	fine	th	them
ng	sing	ū	cute
ô	law	zh	usual
ō	so		

Writing Checklist

1. I followed the directions for writing.

2. My writing shows that I read and understood the article.

3. I capitalized the names of people.

4. I capitalized the proper names of places and things.

5. I put a punctuation mark at the end of each sentence.

6. I read my writing aloud and listened for missing words.

7. I used a dictionary to check words that didn't look right.

Use the chart below to check off the things on the list that you have done.

√ Checklist Numbers	Lesson Numbers								
	1	2	3	4	5	6	7	8	9
1.									
2.									
3.									
4.									
5.									
6.									
7.									

Progress Graph Instructions and Sample

You can take charge of your own progress. The Progress Graph on the next page can help you. Use it to keep track of how you are doing as you work through the lessons in this book. Check the graph often with your teacher. Decide together whether you need to work some more on any of the skills. What types of skills cause you trouble? Talk with your teacher about ways to improve your understanding of these skills.

A sample Progress Graph is shown below. The first three lessons have been filled in to show you how to mark the graph.

Sample Progress Graph

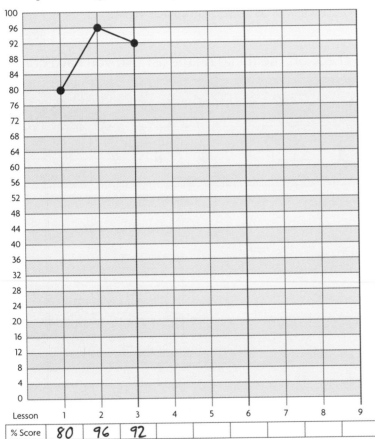

Lesson	1	2	3	4	5	6	7	8	9
% Score	80	96	92						

Progress Graph

Directions: Write your percentage score for each lesson in the box under the lesson number. Then draw a dot on the line to show your score. Draw the dot above the number of the lesson and across from the score you earned. Graph your progress by drawing a line to connect the dots.

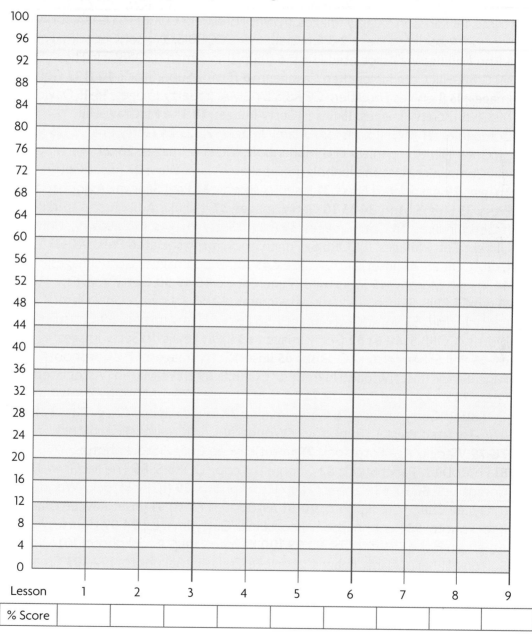

% Score									

Image Credits

Cover (bkgd t)Cartesia/Getty Images, (l)Royalty-Free/CORBIS, (r)Stockbyte/
Punchstock Images, (b)Brand X/SuperStock; **i** Cartesia/Getty Images;
iii (t)David McGlynn/Getty Images, (b)Stockbyte/PunchStock; **iv** Courtesy
American Honda Motor Co.; **v** Bloomimage/CORBIS; **1** (bkgd)Getty Images,
(tr)Mikael Karlsson/Alamy Images, (l)Yves Forestier/CORBIS SYGMA, (br)Paul
Sancya/Associated Press; **2-3** Jim Craigmyle/CORBIS; **3** (inset)Getty Images;
5 Rod Millington/Associated Press; **6** (l)Jim Zuckerman/CORBIS, (r)The
McGraw-Hill Companies/Ken Cavanagh; **8** fStop/SuperStock; **10 11 12** Getty
Images; **13** (l c)Yves Forestier/CORBIS SYGMA, (r)Getty Images; **14-15** David
McGlynn/Getty Images; **15** (inset)Getty Images; **18** The McGraw-Hill
Companies; **21** Mikael Karlsson/Alamy Images; **22 23 24** Getty Images; **25** (l)The
McGraw-Hill Companies/Lisa Mullenholz, (r)Getty Images; **26-27** The McGraw-
Hill Companies/Lisa Mullenholz, (inset sketch) Jami Woy; **27** (inset)Getty
Images; **29** Associated Press; **31** Joseph Murphy; **32** Paul Sancya/Associated
Press; **33** Lois Gibson; **34 35 36** Getty Images; **37** (l)Shakil Adil/Associated Press,
(r)Getty Images; **38** Getty Images; **39** (bkgd)Getty Images, (tr)S. Lowry/Univ
Ulster/Getty Images, (l)CORBIS/PunchStock, (br)Associated Press; **40-41** Tom
Grill/CORBIS; **41** (inset)Getty Images; **43** Altrendo Images/Getty Images;
44 Joseph Murphy; **45** Stockbyte/PunchStock; **48 49 50** Getty Images;
51 (l c)CORBIS/PunchStock; (r)Getty Images; **52-53** S. Lowry/Univ Ulster/
Getty Images; **53** (inset)Getty Images; **56** Pixoi/Alamy Images; **59** Christopher J.
Morris/CORBIS; **60 61 62** Getty Images; **63** (l)Pat Lewis, (r)Getty Images;
64-65 Phil Schermeister/CORBIS; **65** (inset)Getty Images; **67** Goodshoot/
PunchStock, (inset)Visuals Unlimited/CORBIS; **69** Dave Martin/Associated
Press; **70** Associated Press; **72 73 74** Getty Images; **75** (l)Atlantide Phototravel/
CORBIS, (r)Getty Images; **76** Getty Images; **77** (bkgd)Kaycee Craig/iStockphoto,
(tr)Associated Press, (l)Thinkstock/Wonderfile, (br)Creatas/PunchStock;
78-79 VStock/Age Fotostock; **79** (inset)Kaycee Craig/iStockphoto;
81 PhotoDisc/PunchStock; **82** George D. Lepp/CORBIS; **85** The McGraw-Hill
Companies; **86 87 88** Kaycee Craig/iStockphoto; **89** (l)Thinkstock/Wonderfile,
(r)Kaycee Craig/iStockphoto; **90-91** Associated Press; **91** (inset)Kaycee Craig/
iStockphoto; **93** Kent Knudson/PhotoLink/Getty Images; **94 97** Courtesy
American Honda Motor Co.; **98 99 100** Kaycee Craig/iStockphoto; **101** (l)Jeremy
Sutton-Hibbert/Alamy Images, (r)Kaycee Craig/iStockphoto; **102-103** Creatas/
PunchStock; **103** (inset)Kaycee Craig/iStockphoto; **107** Courtesy of The Solid
Waste Agency of Northern Cook County; **108** Toby Talbot/Associated Press;
110 111 112 Kaycee Craig/iStockphoto; **113** (l)Creatas/PunchStock, (r)Kaycee
Craig/iStockphoto; **114** Kaycee Craig/iStockphoto; **115** Brand X/SuperStock
Images; **116** Royalty-Free/CORBIS; **117** Stockbyte/Punchstock Images;
Back Cover Cartesia/Getty Images.